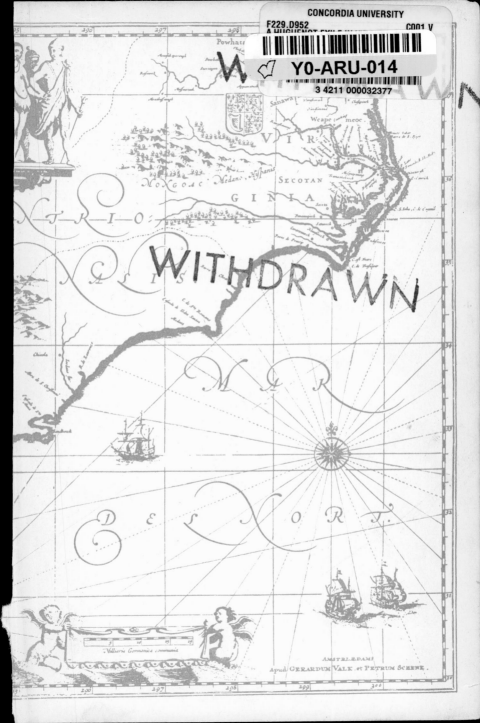

A
HUGUENOT EXILE
IN VIRGINIA

Plate I.   ROSEGILL

A
HUGUENOT EXILE
IN VIRGINIA

or Voyages of
a Frenchman exiled for his Religion
with a description of
Virginia & Maryland

From the Hague Edition of 1687
With an Introduction & Notes
By GILBERT CHINARD

THE PRESS OF THE PIONEERS, INC.
NEW YORK
1934

Printed in the United States of America
by The Stone Printing and Manufacturing Company
Roanoke, Virginia

TABLE OF CONTENTS

VOYAGES OF A FRENCHMAN EXILED FOR HIS RELIGION

ILLUSTRATIONS

INTRODUCTION

THE travel relation of which a complete translation is given here for the first time, has become very rare, and has never been studied especially.[1] On several grounds, however, it deserves to retain the historian's attention. It contains first-hand testimony on the measures taken against the Protestants in the southern provinces of France after the Revocation of the Edict of Nantes, as well as a simple and straightforward account of the flight of a Dauphiné nobleman, his lamentable and sometimes comical Odyssey, until he was able to join in the London "Refuge" his exiled brethren.

If the narrative of the author had gone no further, it would have a distinct if somewhat limited interest. It happened, however, that urged by an adventurous spirit, and eager to settle in a climate which would retain some features of his native Provence, the Huguenot gentleman yielded to the lure of the American mirage. He crossed the ocean; on foot, on horseback, in a boat he

---

[1]For an edition of the French text see Historical Documents. Institut Français de Washington. Cahier V. *Un Français en Virginie.* Avec une introduction et des notes par Gilbert Chinard. Paris: E. Droz—Baltimore: The Johns Hopkins Press. 1932.

travelled through tidewater Virginia, explored the Chesapeake Bay and then, after coming back from his voyages to remote lands, he undertook to communicate to his fellow refugees the results of his observations as well as the plan formed by several Virginia proprietors to receive them. In order to be of assistance to his brethren he consequently published, under circumstances later to be ascertained, a naïve account of his dangers and trials, and his conclusions on the lands he had visited. Having no literary ambition, not attempting to be complete, describing only what he had seen, he cannot be compared with Robert Beverley who, twenty years later, was to present a much more elaborate picture of Virginia. It remains, however, that the French traveler has given us one of the most picturesque and lively descriptions of life in an English colony at the end of the seventeenth century. To the American readers, and particularly to those interested in the study of international psychology, it will prove a very curious document on the state of mind of a European, a Frenchman of two and a half centuries ago, suddenly transplanted into a new civilization. Without being absolutely the first French account of the British colonies, the *Description de la Virgine,* published at The Hague in 1687, will help one to understand how arose and developed, first among the Huguenot exiles, then among the "Philosophes," and finally in the public, this vision of a transatlantic Promised Land, which Providence had

[10]

endowed with all its gifts and seemed to have placed aside, to make it the "last refuge of Liberty."[1]

---

[1]This book has been utilized by Charles W. Baird, in the *History of the Huguenot Emigration to America*, New York (1885), 2 volumes. More recently, a selection of some chapters was published under the title of *A Frenchman in Virginia*, by a "Virginian." Privately printed (1923). Most of the American historians, however, seem to have ignored this very rare document. Mr. Philip Alexander Bruce, the learned author of the *Economic History of Virginia in the Seventeenth Century* (1896), 2 volumes, does not mention our relation. I gave to it a few pages in my study on the *Refugiés Huguenots en Amérique*, Paris (1925), but a more thorough study and some complementary information generously communicated by the too modest "Virginian," have led me to modify on several points the conclusion I had previously reached.

I

DURAND OF DAUPHINÉ

ACCORDING to the indication at the end of the volume, the printing of the VOYAGES/D'UN/FRANÇOIS/ Exilé pour la/Religion/ Avec/ Une Description de la/ VIRGINE & MARILAN/ DANS L' AMERIQUE. A LA HAYE. Imprimé pour l'Autheur. 1687.

was completed on July 7th, 1687.

The only precise information we possess on the author is included in his introduction. He belonged to the noble stock of the Durand of Dauphiné, but all efforts to identify him with known members of this family have proved fruitless. According to Baird, he probably was the "brother" of René de Durand, a gentleman established near Die, in Dauphiné, about twenty leagues east of La Voulte, who, having built a church on his estate, had his property confiscated, his house razed to the ground, and took refuge in Switzerland at the time of the Revocation. As René de Durand himself is known only through our writer, from whom Baird borrowed the above information, our knowledge of the antecedents of our hero remains very incomplete.

Durand de Dauphiné, since such was the name by which he chose to be designated, was of an adventurous disposition and, as this vagabond humor was, according to him, his least reprehensible fault, we may surmise without injustice that he was a somewhat hot-headed youth. He had travelled in France and Italy when, in 1655, at the head of a band of twenty-five or thirty young men he joined the Vaudois who had taken refuge in the valleys of Piedmont after the expedition directed against them by the Duke of Savoy. Finding war to his taste, he participated in "some other campaigns" until somewhat subdued by his experiences he retired to his native Provence, where he had acquired some property. There he married and, after the birth of a daughter and the death of his wife, he had completely settled down, content to spend peacefully in his retreat his remaining days, thanking the Lord for the comfort of his small castle and enjoying the good wine and the good cheer of Provence. The Revocation of the Edict of Nantes was to put an end to this bourgeois happiness. At first Durand had thought that Provence would be spared, for only a few Protestants were to be found there. In October, 1685, he had to accept the evidence of his own eyes. The soldiers of the King were advancing, and on the 18th of the same month, Durand decided to leave his peaceful home. He had his three horses ready and, accompanied by a valet and a boy, he left his dear retreat just as the first dragoons wrapped in their yellow coats, appeared on the slopes of the distant hills. The Odyssey of the refugee was about to begin.

II

THE ESCAPE

ALONG the roads of Provence, travelling at night and hiding in the woods during the day, sometimes meeting with soldiers who filed past him, sometimes resting at places whose inhabitants had recanted and accepted under duress to abjure their religion, slowly and in constant fear, Durand wends his way to Marseilles. Arriving on October 25th, he was to stay three months in the city, hardly daring to go out before dark and spending the night "in the most secluded places." There he heard of the destruction of his house, and, worst of all, that his daughter, who had married an officer in the King's regiment, had been converted, as well as many of his acquaintances. He saw passing slowly through the streets the procession of young Huguenots sentenced to the galleys, heads shorn and in chains, led by soldiers to the harbor. It was the order of the King to remain in the kingdom, but it was the order of the Lord to make every effort to leave the horrible "Babylon" which France had proved to be. If he wished to keep his faith, his clear duty was to leave his country and to become an exile. Pretending to be a Catholic anxious to go on a pilgrimage to Rome, he succeeded in obtaining passage aboard a ship bound for Leghorn, where he landed on January 25, 1686, with his valet and the young "boy" who had followed him in his flight.

There he spent eight or nine days exploring the city, admiring the coaches with the richly clad gentlemen and the beautiful ladies coming from Pisa and Lucca to see the Carnival, and at all times watching his chance to board a boat bound for England. Curiously enough, the Huguenot refugee was helped in his enterprise by a Spanish monk who was perfectly aware of his condition, and through him he obtained free passage on an English boat "coming from Antioch and going to London." Durand was pleasantly surprised to find so much humanity in a man who not only had preserved a grateful memory of the reception he had been tendered by some Protestants of the South when he had been sent there to appear in a law-suit for his convent, but who also went as far as to declare that even in Rome many good souls deplored seeing the Huguenots so rigorously treated. This will not be the only occasion on which Durand will be helped by Catholics and will pay tribute to their charitable attitude.

He was very humane himself, although without sentimentality, and in a similar way he undertook to assist a poor woman from Languedoc who, in order to keep her religion, had decided, alone and with very little money, to venture to seek refuge in England or Holland. He gave her his room on the boat, accepted to let her pass as his wife in order to avoid any ill-natured comment. On every side help was forthcoming, and one of the English merchants with whom he had become acquainted at Leghorn made him the precious gift of forty bottles of Florence muscatel. And so was verified the promise of the Gospel, that "the Lord brings forth friends and consolations in our afflictions."

Durand, however, had not seen the end of his trials. Sailing from Leghorn on February 6th, he was to land in England two months later. The only pleasant episode of the voyage was a short stop at Malaga. The gentlemen in black garments with long swords at their sides, and on their heads hats with brims two feet wide, the ladies wrapped in black silk coats which covered them from head to foot, and hiding their faces behind their mantillas so that hardly one eye could be seen—this was so new and curious that Durand almost forgot his misfortunes. Being a Protestant, he was little interested in churches, but in Malaga he appreciated as a real connoisseur "this good Spanish wine, white and claret, so well known throughout Europe, and even in America."

Nothing was lacking to make the voyage an exciting experience: Turkish pirates met before Tangiers, a terrible storm which forced the ship out of her course just as land was in sight, while part of the cargo shifted

[17]

and threatened them with destruction, the carousing of a young English lord returning from Rome and indulging in too much claret, and finally the illness of the poor woman rescued by Durand. All this is told in a simple, conversational style, not entirely devoid of charm.

On the last day of March, Durand finally landed at Gravesend and, leaving his companions behind him, made haste to London.

Ignorant of the language, and having no address to go to, he roamed about the city until almost dead from fatigue before he could find a lodging where he could bring his "poor sick people." But all was forgotten two days later, "which was a Sunday," when after entering several English churches, he finally discovered the French church and arrived in time for the first preaching. The exile had found the "Refuge," he could now join with his brethren and give the Lord his most humble thanks for his happy arrival "in this fortunate country where truth may be preached without any obstacle or difficulty."

This narrative of Durand's escape is particularly valuable as direct and personal accounts of the great exodus of the French Huguenots are comparatively rare. But the first part of his memoirs deserves attention even more from its human than from its purely historical interest. Up to this point, however, his fortune had not been very different from the experiences of thousands of Huguenots who, during the years immediately preceding the Revocation had, through numberless dangers, abandoned their ancestral homes. Most of them, as we know through many historical studies, found in neighboring countries a refuge and a livelihood. A comparatively large number whose history is not so well known, crossed the seas, settled in strange lands and contributed to the formation of new nations. Of the difficulties they had to overcome, the anxieties that tortured them, the inducements they received from emigration societies, we are still badly informed. On this ground the little book of Durand may be considered as a unique document.

III

THE AMERICAN MIRAGE

MORE fortunate and more foresighted than many of his co-religionists, Durand had been able to prepare for his exile and to gather some money. Having no real anxiety about the near future, and even being able to assist the poor widow from Languedoc, who continued to pass as his wife, he could have made some small establishment in London and spent his last days, if not in luxury, at least in comparative ease. But in the rainy, foggy climate of England, in the damp, coarse atmosphere of London, the Provençal accustomed to the pure air of his mountains and to the sky "clear and always serene" of Southern France, could not breathe freely. His sea voyage and the sight of a new country had reawakened in him a taste for adventure and strange lands. While on the ship he had read a few pamphlets on the British colonies in which, during the last fifty years, a small rivulet of immigrants had percolated. Since he could not go back to his beloved Provence, he would at least endeavor to settle in a country where the soil, the climate and the natural productions would enable him to live again the happy life he had enjoyed in his native country.

He had some money, he was accompanied by a good servant, a healthy, hard worker, and the poor widow who knew how to cultivate silk worms, and had promised to keep house for him. In these regions, which were represented as a New Canaan, life would be easy and pleasant, and so even before landing in England the meridional imagination of Durand had been inflamed and his head was already filled with visions of the lands across the sea.

It would be an interesting study to inquire into the literature of the Huguenot emigration and the publicity contrived to induce the refugees to leave Europe and settle in the New World. I have already called attention to some of these publications; undoubtedly many more could be found.[1] The case of Durand is a striking example of the effect of this propaganda. His arrival in London coincided with a new effort on the part of the great land-owners of Carolina to attract to the colony refugees skilled in "ye manufacture of silkes, oyles and wines."[2] The Protestant minister, Rochefort, had added

---

[1] *Les Réfugiés Huguenots en Amérique.* Paris, Les Belles-Lettres (1925); see particularly Chapter IV, "La publicité et la propagande de l'émigration." Consult also Charles Weiss, *History of the French Protestant Refugees,* Edinburgh and London (1854).

[2] Arthur Henry Hirsch, *The Huguenots of Colonial South Carolina,* Duke University Press (1928). Unfortunately, Mr. Hirsch has treated very succinctly the preliminaries of the emigration.

in 1681 to his *Histoire Naturelle et Morale des Iles Antilles* a supplement of forty-three pages, entitled, "Récit de l'Estat présent des célèbres colonies de la Virginie, de Marie land et de la Caroline." As early as 1684, there had been published in French a brief *Récit de la Province de Pennsylvania* written by William Penn. Many immigrants, isolated or in groups, had arrived in the southern colonies of America, and the proprietors had welcomed these colonists of undeniable moral worth and industry.

This propaganda, which was continued for several decades and is found throughout the first third of the eighteenth century, did not bring immediately the results which might have been expected. The refugees at first refused to believe that the measures taken against them were permanent. A new king, a more liberal policy would probably some day enable them to return to France. Many shared in the hope expressed by M. du Bourdieu, the old minister from Montauban who, although seventy years old, did not intend to die before preaching again in Montpellier. They were strengthened in this belief by the famous *Accomplissement des Prophéties, ou la Délivrance de l'Eglise,* published in Rotterdam in 1686 by the celebrated Jurieu who had predicted the reëstablishment of the Reformed Church in France for the year 1689. But Durand could not be stopped by such considerations. Hardly a few weeks after his arrival he had only one thought in mind: to equip himself as soon as possible for the great adventure. He finally struck a bargain with a captain for twenty écus per person, plus twenty shillings in order to have two beds for his sick companions and a corner in the main cabin where he might place a pallet. As for the food, it was better not to mention it—some poor pea soup, salt beef alternating with salted codfish, and nothing to drink but water. Durand had to spend more than fifteen pounds to buy provisions for the crossing. As he arrived in London at the end of March and remained about six weeks in the city, his departure took place approximately at the end of May, 1686. Our traveler was to land in America on September 22nd; it took him nearly four months to cross the ocean.

IV

BOUND FOR THE PROMISED LAND

O N board, Durand experienced at once a very unpleasant surprise. He had expected to cross with a group of six refugees, several of whom spoke English. At the last minute they had refused to embark, wishing to share in the collections made since April to assist the Huguenots. Much to his despair, Durand, in order not to lose the price of the passage he had paid in advance, had to accept to sail without any friends except "his malades"—the poor widow whom he could not leave alone in England, his servant, and the "little boy." The English-speaking passengers were of dubious character. A few historians of the American colonies have endeavored to prove that the deportation of women of lax morality and of criminals was rare. It is certain that the governors as well as the proprietors made efforts to prevent the mass importation of these undesirables. But the system of indentured servants lent itself to obvious abuses. Many scoundrels, men or women, seized this opportunity to leave England, and the police seem to have been willing to shut their eyes on their departure. Living in the promiscuity of the cabin or common room, embarked sometimes against their will, frightened by the dangers of the sea and very uncertain of ever reaching the other shore, these poor people did not behave like ladies and gentlemen. According to Durand, out of sixty passengers there were no less than twelve young scamps "as insolent and bold as any that could be found in England," and twelve prostitutes who were "to be sold by the captain on arriving in Carolina." One may see in his account what their conduct was during the crossing.

On the other hand, in addition to the five or six honest colonists sailing with their families, Durand had the pleasure of meeting on board a somewhat mysterious person, M. Ysné, a man thirty-two or thirty-three years of age, of good figure and intellect, and who spoke French very well. He was to find him again, on another occasion.

Although the passengers had boarded the ship at Gravesend, they were not to begin the crossing until four weeks later. They met with contrary winds in the Channel, and the captain finally decided to wait at Falmouth for more settled weather. Durand seized this opportunity to place the poor woman from Languedoc and his valet in a house on the shore, hoping that they would recover from the fever which undermined their health. Hardly had they disembarked than they had to return hastily to the ship. They finally sailed northward in order to reach the coast of New England and thence follow the coast to Carolina.

Ten weeks after their departure from London the woman whom Durand had assisted died. Three days later it was the turn of the young boy he had brought with him from France. Provisions were exhausted, and the balance of the voyage was a frightful nightmare. Helped by his valet and his housekeeper, and still having some money left, he would have been able to make a modest settlement in the colonies. Now, his only prospect was to land alone in an unknown country, without resources, disheartened, and his health weakened by successive trials. He would have given himself up to despair, if good M. Ysné had not comforted him.

A ship from Barbados brought news which increased his despondency. Carolina was far from being the paradise described by the immigration agents. There was not an acre of good land there. The colonists had died in large numbers, and an epidemic had killed half of the population of Charleston. M. Ysné, losing courage in his turn, decided to abandon his original project. With some of the merchants on board, he took passage on the Barbados ship, intending to land in Maryland. Durand refused to accompany them, fearing not to find any fellow-countrymen in this new colony, while he expected to receive assistance or advice from the Huguenot colonists of Carolina. Feeling more isolated than ever on a ship which an inexperienced master seemed unable to direct, pushed by the wind to the Gulf of Florida and turned back on the high sea at the time they were getting ready to land at Charleston, having nothing to eat except salted beef more than half rotten, deprived of water to the point that three or four passengers died for the lack of a drop, Durand became so depressed that he felt indifferent to thirst and hunger and all the other miseries. More by chance than through any arranged plan, it seems, the ship finally came in sight of land and entered the straits which mark the entrance to Chesapeake Bay. On the 22nd of September they dropped anchor in the Bay of Mobjack, at the mouth of a small stream called North River. When Durand, wanting to land, changed his clothes covered with pitch and tar, he had to "draw in the belt of his breeches sixteen inches."

V

VIRGINIA

DURAND, cast by ill luck and against his will on the shore of Virginia, was to remain in the colony from the 22nd of September, 1686, until the 15th of March, 1687, a little over six months. It took him several months to give up his original project and to cease to consider his Virginia adventure as a new mishap added to previous misfortunes. Little by little, however, and almost unknowingly, he allowed himself to be won over by the country and by the people, and became a sincere and fervent advocate of Huguenot emigration to Virginia. In his head he carried no preconceived plan, and the land was totally unknown to him. He did not expect to find there anyone he knew, and he even seemed ignorant of the fact that for more than half a century some isolated Huguenots had come individually, to settle in different parts of the colony. For this very reason our discoverer was able to observe reality with almost new eyes, and his descriptions present qualities of sincerity and simplicity too often lacking in other travels. The chief merit of Durand in this respect is to have painted a picture, no doubt somewhat incomplete and imperfect, but wholly original, of the parts of Virginia, and those only, that he had visited. Written almost twenty years before Robert Beverley, and almost forty years before the Reverend Hugh Jones, he is the most picturesque, if not the most accurate witness one may consult for a study of colonial life in Virginia at the end of the seventeenth century.

His itinerary can be easily determined. The ship that carried him had been forced to take shelter in the Bay of Mobjack at the mouth of the North River. Durand, waiting for the vessel to be repaired and put in condition to continue the voyage, rented a room a few miles away, from a Frenchman who had settled at New Point Comfort. From New Point Comfort he went by boat to the house of another Frenchman, M. Servent, located at Kiccotan, at the mouth of the James River. From Kiccotan he went on foot northward, travelling six or seven leagues a day; thus he arrived at the mouth of the North River, the very place where, a little less than a hundred years later, Lafayette and Rochambeau were to witness the surrender of Yorktown. He crossed the river just opposite the small fort which had been built on the other bank, then came back to Point Comfort after travelling on foot more than twenty leagues.

On the 17th of December he started again, always on foot, except when a charitable farmer offered him a horse. He crossed the Pianketank River at Turk's Ferry

8995

and reached Rosegill, the estate of Ralph Wormeley, on the Rappahannock River, where the Governor was visiting at the time. He went up the Rappahannock, crossed the river, and reached Port Tobago, where Ralph Wormeley owned a plantation, and after observing the "savages" for a few days, he entered Stafford County and was at the house of Colonel William Fitzhugh at Bedford-in-Stafford on Christmas eve. He then crossed the Potomac, and after spending a day and a night at the house of a gentleman in Maryland, he re-entered Virginia, stopped at the house of a judge, then again at Bedford, and thence regained Point Comfort, where he expected to find a ship to take him back to Europe. As he did not sail until March 15th, he spent almost two months and a half living in the miserable room he had rented from an inhabitant, collecting information on the country and receiving from the colonists numerous offers of lands for sale.

Durand has set down the result of his observations in four chapters inserted in the middle of his relation. These will be discussed later. Before undertaking this study, it is not out of place to pay some attention to the most significant episodes of his brief exploration of Virginia. Besides the Governor, who was then Lord Howard of Effingham, our refugee had the good fortune to meet two of the men who could be considered as the most famous in the colony: Ralph Wormeley, the owner of Rosegill, and Colonel William Fitzhugh.

On the banks of the Rappahannock, Wormeley had built one of the largest and most elegant colonial mansions of the seventeenth century, which even to-day, after being restored with discretion, is rightly considered as one of the gems of colonial architecture. Besides the main mansion, Rosegill included several subsidiary or secondary buildings forming a real village, surrounded with trees of the primeval forest and ornamented by the rose garden that had given the estate its name. The view reproduced here may convey some idea of the simplicity of the style and of the luxuriant vegetation. On the main floor was a gallery at each end of which was a staircase giving access to five large rooms on the second floor. On the second story, in a sort of enormous attic, fifteen beds could be placed for guests. The reception room on the first floor, the library, the dining room with mahogany panels and delicate carvings, the huge windows opening on the river, are even to-day an impressive sight. It takes but little imagination to reconstruct the whole scene when, on December 19, 1686, Durand came to pay his respects to the Governor, Lord Howard of Effingham, and the great clock adorning the room struck five, at the very time "the last rays of the setting sun were lighting the window-panes."[1] Wormeley, who had been educated

---

[1] See page 104. Many books have been published on the colonial mansions of Virginia. One may refer to the most recent, Paul Wilstach, *Tidewater Virginia*, Indianapolis (Bobbs-Merrill Company), 1929.

at Oxford, owned a very good library, lived in luxury, had no less than twenty-six black slaves and twenty indentured servants working on the plantation. He was able to receive not only the Governor, but also the members of the General Court and numerous friends. Among these people the fare was heavy and the drinking still heavier. White wine from Spain, claret wine from Portugal, cider and beer were generously served. When the supper was over they gambled sometimes throughout the night. This was an America very different from New England, and the southern colonists had none of the Puritanical cant of their northern cousins.

Rosegill was not the only plantation of Ralph Wormeley. Higher on the Rappahannock he owned immense territories on which he planned to organize a regular colony, and he also had an already prosperous plantation twenty-two leagues away from Rosegill. This was Port Tobago, which he took great pleasure in showing to Durand. It was there that Durand had an opportunity to observe the only "savages" he met during his journey. Rather numerous in Virginia in the sixteenth century, the Indians, almost exterminated by epidemics and wars with the colonists, had been progressively pushed back to the West. Near the sea and on the rivers where they were formerly settled only a few lamentable survivors remained, sheltered in poor huts made of reeds and clay. They did not inspire terror or pity, hardly a little curiosity, and our traveller, who had neither the enthusiasm nor the style of Chateaubriand, did not recognize in them the noble children of Nature that the French travellers had celebrated in their relations. But without a few Indians, even if they were "ignoble savages," his picture would not have been complete.

From Port Tobago, as we have seen, Durand went to the Potomac and visited the plantation owned by Colonel William Fitzhugh at Bedford. Although the party included twenty horsemen, the Colonel had such accommodations that he "was not inconvenienced in the least way." After supper, served with the regular accompaniment of good wine and all sorts of drinks, Durand attended one of those entertainments which the rich planters used to give to their guests. They called three fiddlers, a jester and a tumbler, and before the huge fireplace where they had put in no less than a cartload of wood, all the company enjoyed themselves "as much as they could wish."

These sketches of colonial life so frequent in Durand's relation should suffice to warrant him a place by himself among the annalists of old Virginia. It is all too seldom that such personal touches and direct observations are to be found in the documents, or even in the letters of the time. The description of the marriage which he attended is painted with even more vivid colors. A good refugee, from Abbeville, after serving as an indentured worker, and having saved some money, was to marry a young Virginia girl. The account books published in the collection of archives verify the accuracy of Durand's description, but no dry enumeration of the amount of drink and meat consumed on these occasions can produce as strong an impression as this two-page narrative, in which the sober Provençal hardly conceals his astonishment, and almost his terror, at the strange concoctions to which they gave the name of "ponch."

Of all the remarkable characters met in Virginia by Durand, the most curious probably was "Milord" Parker, who, in fact, was already an old acquaintance. Much to Durand's surprise he recognized under this name the young Englishman who had embarked at Dover as M. Ysné, and who, soon after his arrival in the colony, was discovered to belong to a noble English family. After resuming his title he had won the friendship and protection of the Governor, of Ralph Wormeley, and of Colonel Fitzhugh, and the young man who had modestly represented himself as the agent of London merchants, made a fine appearance among the Virginia gentlemen. The change in his fortune and condition had not made him forget the poor gentleman from Dauphiné with whom he had so long and so frequently conversed during the sea voyage. "Milord" Parker had invited Durand to join him at Rosegill and had introduced him to Ralph Wormeley, William Fitzhugh and the gentlemen of the neighborhood. At this point is inserted the most romantic episode of Durand's relation. While at Rosegill, on a fine December day, while Parker was walking sadly along the road that followed the Rappahannock, he confessed to Durand the long succession of errors that had induced him to change his name, and to attempt to make a new fortune in a remote colony. While he was in Provence, a few years before, he had met a beautiful siren, whose lover, in despair at not being able to obtain her hand, had just become a Trappist. The young Englishman did not meet with such insuperable obstacles, and without much ado the beautiful Provençale accepted his love. She apparently had little virtue, a great taste for luxury, and lived like a queen, with her mother in the "hôtel" rented for her in Lyons, by the noble foreigner. But provincial life could not long satisfy Mlle. de la Garenne, and the interesting trio soon went to Paris. In a few months the last remnant of Lord Parker's fortune had vanished. The two lovers, with tears in their eyes, decided to part, so that the young Englishman might procure the money necessary to comply with the demands of the beautiful lady; consequently, he sailed for Virginia, leaving Mlle. de la Garenne the forty *louis* that remained at the bottom of his purse—not without her swearing that she would remain secluded in a convent for the rest of her days rather than give her love to another man. In spite of her letters filled with impassioned declarations, the perfidious one had not kept her word. Even before leaving for America, the unfortunate lover had heard that "the Archbishop of Paris, having fallen in love with her, kept her in a magnificent way." With an abnegation or a lack of courage worthy of Abbé Prévost's Chevalier des Grieux, "Milord" Parker consoled himself in the thought that, having only forty pistoles, she would finally have fallen in penury, but the good prelate would not let her want for anything.

On this curious note the story of Lord Parker comes to an end. One sees easily what use the Abbé Prévost would have made of it, and how movingly he would have portrayed this little adventuress, who may be considered as the elder sister of Manon Lescaut. In spite of Durand's awkward style, the story has such a literary appearance that I hesitated at first to accept it as authentic. The temptation is great to see in it only an embellishment intended to hold the interest of the reader and, at the same time, to flatter the anti-Catholic sentiments of the Huguenots. If one remembers, however, that when Durand was writing, the Archbishop of Paris was the famous Harlay de Champvallon, whose love affairs with Madame de Lesdiguières and many others were well known to the Court, the story of Mlle. de la Garenne becomes less unbelievable. This "good prelate" who, according to Mme. de Grignan, "could only be reproached with his life and his death," was quite capable of keeping more magnificently than secretly the young Provençale.[1]

Furthermore, Lord Parker truly existed.[2] In fact, he was only a baronet and not a lord, but any noble Englishman was "Milord" for a seventeenth century Frenchman. Born in Sussex in 1655, he might have passed for approximately thirty-two or thirty-three years of age in 1686. As the domain on which he lived in England was not far from the estate of Lord Howard of Effingham, one readily understands how his true identity might be discovered by a servant of his Excellency. It seems extraordinary that Durand should have told and published so bluntly the confidences he had been entrusted with on the banks of the Rappahannock, and should not have changed at least the name of the handsome Englishman. He probably would have felt

---

[1]On Harlay de Champvallon (1625–1695), appointed Archbishop of Paris in 1667, see Saint-Simon, Vol. II, pp. 349–354 (Boislile ed. 1879). One should also consult the article of M. Georges Goyau in the *Catholic Encyclopedia,* where is found the judgment of Father Armand Jean, according to whom, "his attitude in the Assembly of the Clergy was reprehensible, and he was not less blameworthy in his private life." Finally one should not forget the page in which, following Saint-Simon, Maurice Barrès paints Harlay de Champvallon and Mme. de Lesdiguières walking slowly in the garden of Conflans, while gardeners follow them at a distance, to rake out the traces of their steps on the sand. (*Du Sang, de la Volupté et de la Mort.*)

[2]The "Virginian" translator of *A Frenchman in Virginia,* believes that Durand had met Sir Robert Parker (1655–1691), baronet of Ratton in Sussex, and quotes from Burke's *Extinct Baronetcies,* and G. E. C. *Complete Baronetage.*

more hesitation in dealing with a fellow Huguenot; but Parker was a Catholic, and it was too splendid an occasion to hit the prelate for whom the Protestant exile could feel no sympathy. In this particular case, as in so many others, once more life has anticipated literature. The young Englishman who dreams in a melancholy fashion on the banks of an American river, and cannot forget the unfaithful one whom he has not the courage to hate, reminds us forcibly, if not of Chateaubriand, at least of Abbé Prévost. In this historical character can be distinguished some of the traits which later were to move so deeply romantic sentimentality.

VI

PROPAGANDA AND COLONIZATION

DURAND had not given up his trip to Carolina in order to enjoy himself or to sympathize with a romantic lover. Since his arrival, he had been hunted by landowners offering to sell tracts on which the Huguenots could settle. Perhaps Lord Parker himself, although a Catholic, was not unaware of the plans which were then formed to attract to Virginia colonists of high morality and industrious workers who would have brought along with them the arts and trades that the indentured servants were not capable of exercising, and that the aristocratic Virginians would have considered as beneath their rank.

On the other hand, Durand arrived at a time when, according to the *Cohabitation Act* of 1680, a strong effort was being made by the authorities of the colony to group the inhabitants into "towns," so as to facilitate the exchange of products and the development of "manufactures." As early as 1680, an act had authorized the creation of a "town" in Middlesex, west of the plantation on which lived Ralph Wormeley. This "town" received the name of Urbana in 1705 and still

[39]

exists to-day.[1] But many were the "towns" for which tracts of land were set aside and names given to, but which were never settled except on paper.

But the most enterprizing of these promoters was certainly Colonel William Fitzhugh. At the beginning of 1686 he had registered in Stafford County an enormous tract of 21,996 acres of land, which later received the name of Ravensworth. In a curious document, published in the *Landmarks of Old Prince William*, he invited the French Protestants to settle there.[2] One hundred and fifty or two hundred families could easily form an establishment, and the prices were most moderate: seven pounds sterling for a hundred acres or twenty shillings if one preferred to pay rent. In addition, Fitzhugh promised to provide the settlers, at a minimum price, with meat and corn during the first year, and to sell them anything they might need. He ended with a consideration to which Protestants from the south of France could not remain indifferent. These he had especially in view when he declared that this land was particularly suited for the cultivation of grapevines. One may well believe that the enterprizing Colonel did not miss the opportunity to do some publicity work with Durand, and to paint an enticing picture of all the

[1]William Waller Hening, *Virginia Statutes at Large,* Richmond (1812), Vol. II, p. 473.
[2]*Landmarks of Old Prince William.* A Study in Northern Virginia. Richmond (1924), The Old Dominion Press. 2 Vols. Privately Printed. *See* Vol. I, p. 188.

advantages that the French Protestants could not fail to find in Stafford County.

It was not the only project in which Fitzhugh was interested. One of his trusted friends, Samuel Hayward, brother of Nicholas Hayward, notary public on the Virginia walk of the Exchange at London, sought for his part to establish a colony of French refugees near Bedford. The 10th of January, 1686, after long negotiations, he succeeded in forming a society composed of Richard Foote, Robert Bristow and George Brent, of Woodstock, in order to establish a "town" which was authorized by a Royal Edict of February 10th. The new "town" was to bear the name "Brenton" or "Brentown" and promise was made that the inhabitants should exercise fully their religion without being disturbed or molested.[1]

It is more than likely that it was one of these associates who went to call on Durand when he was in Stafford County.[2] This hypothesis becomes almost a certainty if one goes back to the *Propositions* for Virginia," signed by Nicholas Hayward, London representative of the Brenton company, and published by Durand at the end of his relation.[3]

---

[1]The Correspondence of William Fitzhugh has been published in the *Virginia Magazine of History and Biography*, new series, Vols. I, II, III (1893 *et seq.*). Most of the letters on this project will be found in Vol. I, pp. 391 *et seq.*

[2]See p. 159.

[3]See p. 179.

Even when Durand, having ended his survey, was waiting for the ship which was to take him back to Europe, he received further calls from owners of lands offering sometimes two thousand acres, and other times a thousand acres, while some were simply attempting to get rid of tracts of land of seven hundred, five or four hundred acres.[1]

Although on some occasions Durand could rightly complain of having been exploited by the inhabitants, one sees that all things considered, and during the greater part of his journey he was taken in hand by people who had a real interest in treating him well and in showing him things under their most favorable aspect. This may be said without doing injustice to the genuine hospitality of the Virginians of the seventeenth century. Almost never was he left alone. People showed him only what they wanted him to see. They tried to convert him to the cause of Virginia colonization, particularly at the beginning of his stay, when he was still considering Carolina. When he sailed back, the proprietors had won their cause. Durand had decided to praise to his brethren the choice of Virginia, and to advise them against settling in Carolina. It is rather amusing to see that in spite of the enthusiastic tone of his narrative, neither Nicholas Hayward nor William Fitzhugh was entirely satisfied with it, so difficult is it to please people who have land to sell! As

[1] See p. 164.

soon as the small book of the refugee came to the hands of Nicholas Hayward, he sent a copy of it to his associate, who, in a letter dated June 1, 1688, answered that he agreed absolutely with Hayward, that Durand's book was "a most weak impolite piece, having neither the Rules of History nor method of description and taking it only as a private Gentleman's Journal, 'tis as barren and defective there too."[1]

On this occasion Fitzhugh evidenced real ill grace. Incomplete and imperfect as an historical relation as Durand's account may have been, it was in fact admirably calculated to attract the attention of the French refugees to Virginia. It was first of all a work of propaganda and of publicity, and it is from that aspect that it must be considered.

---

[1] *Virginia Magazine*, January, 1895, Vol. II, p. 270.

VII

THE NEW CANAAN

DURAND was too honest to undertake deliberately to deceive his coreligionists. He concealed none of the horrors of the crossing, the lack of honesty of the captain who carried the immigrants, the greed of certain inhabitants of Gloucester County who, poor themselves, were exceedingly hard on strangers. But with these reservations, he nevertheless described Virginia as a Promised Land, and a true Utopia. As he intended to supply the refugees with all possible information he devoted three chapters to what may be called the description proper, although much practical information is scattered throughout the narrative.

It is hardly necessary to remark that his knowledge of geography is very rudimentary, or to call attention to the curious sentence in which he seems to indicate that Peru is just on the other side of the Virginia mountains.[1] We should look for an account, not of the whole of Virginia, but of what he has seen, of this region watered by "three large rivers where the effect of the

---

[1]See p. 104.

tide is felt far inland"—tidewater Virginia. It was the most productive and the richest region, in which had settled the great proprietors, who formed a colonial aristocracy. There, winter was shorter and more temperate, and when the wind stopped blowing it resembled the spring of France. The country was so good and so fertile that if one had only "fifty acres of land, two valets, and a maid," he had nothing to do except to visit the neighbors, to hunt, and to enjoy the gifts of Providence. The inhabitants were so lazy that they imported everything from England, and there was not a woman who knew how to spin. The Huguenots might well believe that French people, accustomed to working so hard in order to pay the taxes with which the king had burdened them, could not fail to make there a rapid fortune.

In his enthusiasm, Durand denounced even his native Provence, the mountains of which offered only "a hideous perspective" with stones, rocks and sterile soil barren of woods or grass. Virginia, on the contrary, was like a beautiful orchard, watered by pleasant streams, with fine meadows and fields so fertile that it was not even necessary to plough them.

In this idyllic land the happy Virginians had built houses, if not beautiful, at least very comfortable. The forests were full of all sorts of game, the cattle roamed at liberty in the meadows and the woods, flocks of ducks and wild geese flew over the marshes, and a wonderful little bird, no bigger than a fly, with feathers reflecting the colors of the rainbow, came to sip honey from the flowers in the gardens. Fruit trees grew with an extraordinary rapidity, grapevines covered whole acres of land, and French families knowing how to prune them would certainly make a great profit.

In conclusion, Durand found no less than five considerations for which Virginia was preferable to Carolina, and four reasons for declaring the superiority of this colony over the northern colonies; but of all the regions of Virginia he visited, none could equal the counties of Rappahannock and Stafford. There pleasantness, health and fertility were united. Over the country were distributed plains and hills, and one could have at the same time fine meadows and fine vineyards, "for wine never comes naturally in the plains." The climate was particularly healthy and Durand saw with satisfaction that the inhabitants of these parts of Virginia had more "embonpoint" than elsewhere, and a better and more lively complexion.

In these conclusions no restriction remains. All of the shadows have disappeared from the picture. Virginia is shown in an idyllic light. It has become the Promised Land of the French exiled for their religion. Whatever may be the number of refugees in London, and although two hundred arrive there every day, and even supposing that all the Protestants who, in order to remain in France have recanted, should repent and join their brethren, there would still be land enough in Virginia for everyone. Houses cost almost nothing to build, except a few nails. For thirty or forty pistoles one could buy a hundred acres of the best fields, and if one had no money and were forced to borrow, all debts could be paid after the first crop of tobacco. This was a marvellous vision, and well suited to attract the poor people who, after encountering a thousand trials, led in London a most precarious existence.

It may perhaps be asked why Durand did not stay in this land of plenty, but chose to face once more the dangers of the sea in order to go back to London, where he was expected by neither friends nor family. The reasons he gave are quite plausible and enable one to get a deeper insight into the psychology of the refugees. However attractive Virginia may have been, French people resided there only in very small numbers. To live among men speaking a foreign language, and particularly to give up religious service in French, was for Durand an unbearable prospect. Furthermore, before sailing he had bought a copy of the little book in which M. Jurieu, the great minister of the refugees, promised the reëstablishment of the reformed religion in France for the year 1689.[1] Durand did not wish to die before being a witness of the restoration of the religion in his country, as he had witnessed its dissolution and ruin. This last consideration enables one to understand why

[1]See p. 162.

the account of *"Virgine et Marilan"* did not determine a new orientation in Huguenot immigration. In spite of all the efforts of recruiting agents, in spite of the promises of Nicholas Hayward printed at the end of the book, in spite of Durand's affirmation that one could trust the declarations of the Brenton Company and of Mr. Wormeley, the refugees in Holland and London could not all at once give up every hope of ever going back to their native land. They had left France in haste, as one flees to escape a cataclysm, and they hesitated to go far away. They had not been able to sever at one stroke the ancestral bonds which still bound them to the French soil. Their eyes still turned towards the fields of their fathers, and their destroyed homes. Their hopes were kept alive by the word of their ministers, and only the most adventurous crossed the ocean. New England received a comparatively large number, a few isolated immigrants went to Virginia, small groups continued to sail for Carolina, but one must wait until the end of the seventeenth century to see the refugees accept exile as a definite prospect, and undertake to build new homes over the seas in this Virginia which had invited them, and which Durand had described in such attractive colors. It does not seem that he was able to join them. As he was writing his relation, he felt old and weak. His dearest wish, "if God granted him enough strength," was to go back to live among the honest people who had welcomed him so warmly; but his relation was, in fact, a sort of testament in which he bequeathed to the faithful Frenchmen who had escaped from "the captivity of Babylon," the vision and the promise of a new country where they and their children could practice their religion and find again their lost happiness.

CONCLUSION

SUCH are the essential aspects of this curious document which belongs at the same time to French history and to the colonial history of America. Writers looking for a polished style will discover little here to please them, for as Colonel Fitzhugh had written, Durand offered the public "a most weak, impolite piece." Nor will one find here the precise information with figures, so frequently encountered in the old archives which contain precious material for the writing of economic histories. Durand has not even taken pains to describe exactly the form of government then existing in the Old Dominion. If he speaks *en passant* of the judiciary, it is to tell us that the members of the Council arrived on horseback, with boots and spurs, to call on the Governor, and conducted their deliberations with their swords at their sides. On the other hand, one will find here, and without having to look far for it, the portrait of a man who just as frankly as Montaigne confesses his weaknesses and his hopes. He loves wine and good cheer; he loves pleasant landscapes. He discovers no beauty in the tempest and rocks about which the romantic imagination will rave. He would not have asked to be tied to the mast of the ship in order to see the waves break over the bridge, as did Chateaubriand a hundred years later; but with these limitations we must acknowledge that he is far from lacking in interest. He wrote as he spoke, with certain provincialisms, badly constructed sentences in which are scattered locutions that smack of the soil and afford a pleasant change after reading the over-labored and over-burdened productions of other writers. His account has a straightforward and sincere quality too seldom met with in traveller's relations. Above all, one must admire him for not having become embittered or rebellious, for not indulging in violent denunciations, for thinking of others rather than of himself, and for placing in the Lord and in the prophecies of M. Jurieu a naïve trust and a profound faith.

Being a Frenchman, and in addition a Provençal, he was essentially sociable, and was interested in describing the life of society in Malaga, as well as in the New World. Some years ago, Mr. Philip Alexander Bruce expressed the regret that there should be no true account of travel in Virginia in the seventeenth century, and no really personal impressions of colonial life during that period. He would have enjoyed the *Voyage en Virgine et Marilan* of the gentleman from Dauphiné, if this relation had been available when the learned historian wrote his study of *Social Life in Virginia in the Seventeenth Century*. Durand may have been mistaken on some points, but he remains the one French writer and, we may say, the only seventeenth century writer, who has seen and painted from life, with the awkwardness and naïveté of the primitives, a simple picture of colonial Virginia, the charm of which still pervades the sumptuous mansions built by the great proprietors in the midst of the American wilderness, and in the clearings of the primeval forests.

GILBERT CHINARD

Baltimore, May, 1934.

———

NOTE—Hastily printed and not revised by the author, the book of Durand contains many typographical errors. The spelling of the writer has been reproduced in the most typical instances which reveal an amusing effort to transcribe phonetically words he had never seen written.

I wish also to thank here the "Virginian," who translated, a few years ago, a part of Durand's relation; Mr. Henry R. McIlwaine, editor of the Historical Society of Virginia, the late William G. Stanard, whose assistance has been most valuable, and Mr. E. Cook, the Richmond photographer, whose collection of pictures has greatly aided me.

VOYAGES

D'UN

FRANÇOIS

Exilé pour la

RELIGION

AVEC

Une description de la

VIRGINE & MARILAN

dans

L'AMÉRIQUE

A LA HAYE

Imprimé pour l'Autheur, 1687

Plate II.   Title Page (reduced) of 1687 Edition of Durand's Narrative

VOYAGES

of

a Frenchman exiled for his Religion
with a description of Virginia &
Maryland in America

*To all faithful Frenchmen who have escaped from
the captivity of Babylon to follow truth :*

Gentlemen,

HAD the cruelties inflicted upon the Protestants in France not been reported throughout all Europe, & even throughout the
Universe, I might be taxed with levity &
even folly for undertaking journeys to the most remote
countries, when already well advanced in years, being
nowise urged by the desire of acquiring wealth, &
knowing nothing of business; but they are so widely
known that I need say no more. Not that the desire to
travel was the least of the passions of my youth, but as
my private affairs prevented me from satisfying it completely, I had to content myself with seeing France &
part of Italy. My second journey took place in the year

1655. When I heard that those of the poor Vaudois in the valleys of Piedmont who had escaped massacre had risen in arms, I gathered 25 or 30 young men of my own age who chose me as their leader, & we joined them & remained there until four Swiss envoys succeeded in concluding a peace. Later I engaged in some other campaigns, & finally, like many others, I retired. Thus was spent the largest part of my life, & I would have ended it the same way, had God not honored me by calling upon me to suffer for His name.

I was born in the Province of Dauphiné, of the Durans of ancient & noble lineage. The head of this family, René Durand, was among the first to feel the effects of this cruel persecution, as, five years ago, having seen with deep sorrow the Temple of his town razed on the slightest of pretexts, he conducted the worship of God in peasant cottages, & for this reason was not included in the amnesty which the King granted to most of those who had attended it.[1] His houses were given up to the soldiers to be plundered, then razed, & all his property, amounting to an income of ten thousand livres, was confiscated; as for him, he escaped to Switzerland as best he could. I know not whether he is still alive.

As for me, part of my property was at my birth-place, & another part in Provence, where I happened to be when this dreadful tempest broke over our king-

---

[1]On Durand's family see *Introduction*, p. 12.

dom. There only a few peasants were of the Huguenot religion, & I would doubtless have been surprised by the Dragoons, had not three of my relatives from Dauphiné, one a minister seventy-five years old, arrived to take refuge with me, after abandoning their homes & property to the soldiery. They had escaped with great difficulty to the woods, & with even greater difficulty had come to me, travelling twenty leagues afoot, through by-roads. After hearing from them the sad, grievous account of the complete ruin of our Religion in our Province, I began at once to prepare everything for my departure. They had time to rest a few days only, for as soon as it was known that they were there, we were so threatened from all sides that they were forced to leave. They took the road to Orange, which they did not reach, for I discovered the next day that that Principality had been visited with the same punishment. As regards the Pastor, he will have availed himself of the liberty procured through exile. But as for those noble confessors of the faith, I know not what has become of them; I pray that God has granted them, as he did me, the grace to escape.

Now God permitted me, from the day of my flight, which was on the 18th of October, 1685, until the seventh of May, 1687, when I returned anew to London, to see several cities in Italy, six Provinces or Kingdoms of Spain, part of England, to travel over some of the West Indies in America, during which journeys I

traveled, according to the pilot's reckoning, six thous-
and eight hundred leagues by water, not to speak of the
distance I covered on land, walking or on horseback,
having journeyed half the time upon the sea, & the
other half upon land. Upon this element, since God so
willed it, I suffered hunger, thirst, perils, shipwrecks,
& all that man can endure without dying, but I was
blessed with such a robust constitution that although
navigation was unknown to me before I embarked at
Marseilles, I never experienced even the slightest sea-
sickness.

But it would be entirely unnecessary, Gentlemen,
whom I may be allowed to call my very dear Brothers
& Sisters, because of the esteem & affection which
I have for all of you, to discourse upon my travels, if I
aimed only to satisfy the curiosity of a few; on the contrary, I am so aware of my limitations that, had I only
this end in view, I am fully convinced my unpolished
utterances in an age as enlightened as ours, would of-
fend a hundred times more than they would please. I
never learned either periods or rhetoric; my parents intended me to be a soldier, & consequently had me
taught no science other than to read & write, & far
from wishing to make an ostentatious display in my
narrative, God is my witness that had the despondency
brought by so many fatigues, sufferings & afflictions,
permitted me to go to Holland & Germany in order
to inform so many of you orally, poor faithful wanderers

over Europe, of a very favorable refuge in the most beautiful & most fertile country I have yet seen, I would never have been bold enough to allow so many imperfections to see the light: but charity alone has urged me to act, & since we are told in Holy Writ that charity covers a multitude of sins, I hope that it will cover a part of my shortcomings also. I thought at one time of publishing just a description of this country, similar to the pamphlets seen in France regarding Carolina & Pennsylvania[1]; but later I realized that, appearing unsupported, paper being made to say anything, it might with reason be suspected of untruth, for I am obliged in fairness to declare that these same pamphlets wander from the truth in many respects, as I will show in due course.

Therefore I was convinced that I could not give the account of a man who chanced to be there as if he had dropped from the sky, that it was necessary to state the reasons which obliged him to go there, & those which induced him to come back; & for this purpose I have deemed it appropriate to touch lightly upon my travels in Europe, as a number of those for whom I write are more or less acquainted with those countries, & to begin with my escape. I mention my family, not through pride, for I am not unmindful that self-complacency & vainglory are reprehensible in any station,

---

[1]On emigration propaganda see G. Chinard, *Les Réfugiés Huguenots en Amérique,* Paris (1925), Ch. IV, and *Introduction,* p. 39.

& would be absolutely insufferable in that of a poor Refugee like myself; but in order that those of my Province, where my family is rather well known, happening to read this, may bear witness that we are not wont to beget impostors.

Arriving in London, I met a very worthy Minister from our province who, following my accounts of this country, expressed to me his readiness to go there, especially, said he, because there being Infidels, God might well call him to convert them.

It is a special favor of Heaven that our leaders have been spared notwithstanding the fury & enmity of our merciless persecutors, & that we poor refugees have been able to join these illustrious exiles to be encouraged to persevere & to be consoled for all that we have had to abandon, they are the choicest among Pastors to whom we cannot show too much respect & reverence, since God has allowed the tares to be separated from the wheat; they are the true Apostles, sorted & chosen; the Judases have remained in the bosom of Babylon after making themselves known by their scandalous & criminal apostasy. So it will be under their good & wise guidance that I intend, if God grants me enough life & health, to spend the rest of my days in this new world with some of these poor fugitives. What I have written may be accepted in perfect confidence. I have no more interest in praising one country than another, & besides professing to be absolutely truthful, my intention to return there should remove all suspicion. For as I am alone, I would not fear to suffer want in Europe should I wish to remain here; but it is because I am enchanted with the beauty & the fertility of that country. As one might be wearied by the accounts of my travels in Europe, I have made them as brief as possible. I have dwelt somewhat more at length upon those in America, chiefly when speaking of the parts I have visited. For the others, when I have just seen the land, or sailed along the coast, I have related only what I have learned from people worthy of credence.

In my fortune will be seen the wonderful workings of Providence, not that I wish to speak of the aid I received as soon as I was among Protestants; the whole Universe has heard that from the time when they reached Switzerland, Germany, & Holland, far from being in need, the Refugees were not allowed to spend any of the wealth they brought with them, & if the English did not go this far, they nevertheless distributed huge sums among them. On the contrary I received very little; but God has caused to come forth from the nation the most hostile to the Reformation, & naturally the most active against our Religion, men who have rendered me the greatest services, & He has even moved to compassion others of the same communion, that I might receive from them a thousand benefits, this is something not to be found in the des-

tiny of any other Refugee. I shall end, then, my dear
Brothers & Sisters, in begging that instead of pausing
at the imperfections without number you will find in
this little Treatise, you will use some of your charity to
cover them, since had not charity moved & prompted
me, I should never have had the temerity to attempt it.

FIRST VOYAGE

THE JOURNEY TO MARSEILLES

THERE were as yet no soldiers in this Province; it had been left until last, for it had only seven thousand Protestant families. I forthwith gave orders in my neighborhood to apprise me immediately of their arrival. Three days after the departure of these Gentlemen, on the 18th of October, 1685, I learned, towards noon, that some troops had arrived through Tarascon; thereupon I set out instantly, with three horses & two servants, thinking that I should have time to reach Marseilles before they advanced, for I knew there were five or six large towns of six or seven hundred inhabitants each, where there were practically no Papists, & where I was acquainted with wealthy Bourgeois worth a hundred thousand écus, & greatly attached to the Religion. I judged therefore that any of the said towns would keep the Regiment a month before surrendering, but I was greatly surprised late the next day to behold a number of yellow coats wending their way down a low mountain. I then had no doubt that they were Dragoons. I sent my retinue to hide in a valley, for had they seen two horses laden with furniture, & a small boy ten years old, they would surely have suspected my Religion & my flight, hence I would have been in danger, as I was still in our Bishopric, where I had been counted, & felt certain that the Commander would have the roll-call & that I would head it, inasmuch as there were but two Gentlemen of the Religion in the said district, the rest being Peasantry. As for myself, I drew up by the roadside on my fine mount, looking as unconcerned as I could, & watched twelve Companies of Dragoons, making up the Regiment, file past.

When they had marched away, I rode all night in order to get out of the Bishopric, & coming upon some foot-soldiers, I questioned them for news. They answered with indignation, interspersing their remarks with oaths, that they had that day passed through two or three large towns full of Huguenots who had shown so little regard for their Religion that as soon as they heard the drums they had climbed on each others shoulders to enter the Church & recant; that the first town they came to in the Province had indeed resisted three days, & they had profited greatly thereby, whereas in the others they had not been allowed to unsaddle a horse or to take even a single hen. I was surprised at the swiftness of these fine conquests, & as I stood outside of the boundaries of the Bishopric, learning that there were no more soldiers behind, I decided to go for a rest to one of these towns, called Mérindel. The sorry plight of these unhappy people touched me deeply. Their consciences were beginning to reproach them for the crime they had so readily committed. I soon departed & took my subsequent lodgings in places where there were no Protestants. There all the Dragoons had been quartered for fear of the ever ready rebellion of these Protestant towns. They were so accustomed to license & extortion that, beating & torture excepted, they carried on here the same abuses as they did against the Protestants, so that the unfortunate people cursed terribly this hellish enterprise. Thus I kept travelling along deserted roads until I came at last within two leagues of Marseilles. This was on the 25th of October. I was suddenly surrounded by a detachment of a hundred or a hundred & twenty dragoons. I thought then that I should be unable to escape torture & prison, but soon realized they did not mean to arrest me, for they politely inquired the way to Marseilles. I pointed it out & let them file past. I heard later that there were 25 or 30 inhabitants in that great city who had not yet recanted, & they were going to convert them. Thus my fears proved to be groundless. On arriving I also learned from a man of my own village who had recanted, that the day following my departure a company of Dragoons had broken into my house, burned my Bibles & all my sacred books & acted as they are wont to do in the homes of those who have

[63]

escaped. I took my lodgings in secluded places, & during the day I usually stayed in the shops of those who formerly had belonged to the Religion. They helped me, with great kindness, in every way they could, & undertook to find some means of conveying me to England or Holland, but without success. I had tarried there two months, when one of them led me to hope that an English vessel would carry me. I therefore had my furniture packed in a box & put aboard, but three days later the Captain of this ship asked me to please have it taken off, as he was unwilling to transport me because he feared for his own safety. I told him to take the box to London where, if God granted I should go, I would recover it, otherwise, he might do with it as he thought best, for I was convinced that if I removed it I would be discovered.

A man-servant who had served me for fourteen years had become a muleteer, & having changed his Religion, was pursuing his business without fear, in Marseilles. I trusted him, & meeting him a short while after my arrival in that city, I instructed him to come to me on each of his trips. Through him I learned that a daughter I had given in marriage eighteen months before, to a Captain commanding the third battalion of the Regiment of Saut, had recanted, with her husband, & that one of my own brothers & all the nobility in our Province who had remained there had done like-wise, which distressed me greatly; however, I was some-

what comforted to hear that a Gentleman of my neighborhood, with an income of over twelve thousand
pounds, as well as four sisters, young, fair & very
wealthy, had nobly abandoned everything, & fled to
Switzerland. This Gentleman was a first cousin of my
deceased wife, & the young ladies her nieces. He
further told me that four of my first cousins or their
sons, had done the same thing; that a young girl, Mar-
guerite de Durand, seventeen years old, also a daughter
of a first cousin, had likewise attempted to escape,
dressed as a boy, & together with some men met with
an ambuscade as they were about to cross a bridge, &
when they tried to stop her, she killed two men,
wounded two more, & was finally shot through the
body. When it was realized that she was a girl, they
took her to a nearby castle, & I do not know whether
she escaped. In addition, I was warned that, far from
keeping the promise given in the last article of the Edict
of the 22nd of October, those who had gone back trust-
ing its good faith had been treated worse than the
others, until they recanted. I heard also that anyone attempting to leave the country was ruthlessly condemned
to the Galleys; this report was substantiated by the
arrival of twenty-two young men, three or four from
my own town among them, whom I saw shaved &
fettered. All these reasons prompted me to leave the
Kingdom, or rather Babylon. The King forbade it under
penalty of the Galleys, but God commanded it under

pain of having me share in the infliction of His wounds. Therefore, in a matter of such importance, involving nothing less than my salvation, I preferred to obey God rather than the King. I had been three months hiding in this town, where I spent a great deal, the cost of living being always very high, when, unable to find any means of going straight to England or Holland, I went to a skipper & asked him what he would charge to take me immediately to Italy. He wanted twenty guineas, which I promised to give him, & as I needed a health certificate, without which I could not enter any Italian city, I went to one of the Consuls. I changed my name, saying that I was from a town in Provence where there had never been any Protestants, & claimed that I had taken a vow to go to Rome. In this way, although he must have suspected my plan, the skipper took me, with my servant & my boy, out of the port at ten o'clock in the evening, & four days later landed us at Leghorn. This was on the 25th of January, 1686.

SECOND VOYAGE

VOYAGE TO LEGHORN

AS soon as I reached Leghorn I undertook to get acquainted with the French and English Protestant merchants, so that with their help I might get to England. This offered no difficulty, as from the first I received many civilities from everyone. I stopped there for eight or nine days, & indeed I was never bored. Leghorn is a very agreeable city with fine, well-built houses, wide streets, & pavements so clean that one could eat on them; a small city, in truth, but for that very reason so much stronger, for not only does the sea surround it, but there are splendid forts very well built, & new ones are being built all the time. There is a garrison of two thousand men, besides four galleys usually maintained there by the Grand Duke. All who are not on duty are drilled regularly every working-day, on the parade-grounds, the finest & largest I have ever seen. They do not try to save powder, as in France, when practicing, for no musketeer will shoot less than three or four times. In the Bastions are many places where entrance is forbidden. It happened that at the time of my arrival, a young French lord said to be of the house of Bétune, from the army at Venice, where he had served as a volunteer during the campaign, was visiting the forts & insisted upon entering the tunnel of an isolated bastion, against the order of a sentry, who called the corporal. He was manhandled by the watch, & immediately went to headquarters to complain to the governor, who, far from giving him satisfaction or letting him hope for any, told him they had only done their duty. Thereupon, he drew his sword against the governor, but was seized by the guard, put in prison, & three days later beheaded. This was a great humiliation for all the Frenchmen in the city. It was during the last days of Shrove-tide, & as there were some very good comedians in the city, on Saturday twenty coaches arrived & as many open carriages loaded with noblemen & ladies from Pisa & Lucca. Never have I seen people more magnificently dressed.

Five or six days later a fine English merchant vessel going from Antioch to London stopped on her way. Messrs. Othon Bonal & Christophre Parker,[1] very honest English merchants, & Messrs. Mate, French merchants, immediately asked the Captain to take me to England, & by their arguments persuaded him into

---

[1]Christopher. Here, as in many other places, Durand reproduced approximately the pronunciation of words he had never seen written.

discounting half my passage money, of which fact they straightway acquainted me, & I returned to my lodgings. No sooner had I reached there than a Spanish monk accosted me, & taking me into a private room, told me that he had learned I had left France because of the Religion, & intended to go to England, for which purpose I had commissioned these Gentlemen, naming indeed all those merchants, & he went on to say that he had lived in France a fairly long time, & learned the language. He had had a law-suit in Castres, the seat of the Chamber of Led at that time, & the Gentlemen of the Religion had shown him great kindness & courtesy; having found them the most honest people in our kingdom, & being even under great obligations to them, he had since that time always held them in high esteem. He was in Spain when he heard of the mistreatment we suffered, & not only he, but all honest people deplored our misfortunes; at the present time he was returning from Rome, where many good souls likewise sympathized with us, & he was ready to serve me in everything, with his very blood if necessary.[1] He was acquainted with all the Spanish merchants in the city, & knew that some of them were closely connected with the Captain who was to transport me, & he meant to

---

[1]This is a curious confirmation of the lack of enthusiasm of Rome to congratulate Louis XIV on the results of the Revocation. See Louis O'Brien, *Innocent XI and the Revocation of the Edict of Nantes*, Berkeley, California, 1930.

exert himself to secure their assistance in my behalf. Had I not been in a place of safety, I would have been surprised to see a man in a monk's frock so well informed of my affairs, as I had imparted them only to these Merchants. Nevertheless, as he spoke so frankly & seemed quite sincere, I candidly made known to him my plans. The next day Monsieur Matte told me that he was a very honest man, who had been present when they spoke of me to the captain, & they had hidden nothing from him. He made such efforts in my behalf with the Spanish merchants that they obtained from the captain a remission of the other half of the fare, & he came to tell me about it. I thanked him with all my heart, & he professed himself deeply gratified to have done me this service, & I, for my part, was grateful to receive it from a person of such character.

This would not have been surprising from a Dutch vessel. While walking with Monsieur Matte we met the master of a Dutch ship who spoke good French. He told us it would be a month before he could leave, but were I willing to wait, he would transport me free of charge. In fact, many of them have taken people in this way, but the English always demanded payment, & I believe I am the only one who was ever thus conveyed; besides, my box of furniture drew me to England rather than to Holland.

Close by my lodgings lived the widow of a Languedoc bourgeois who came from southern Dauphiné. She had escaped as best she could, with a nephew of her husband. This worthy gentleman, hearing of the Edict of the 22nd of October, & believing he could recover his possessions without molestation because of his religion, had heartlessly abandoned her, & discovering that some tartans from Aigue Morte, after carrying wine from Frontignan to Leghorn, were starting on their return trip, sailed away on one of them. This woman was childless. Her husband had left her the income from a country estate, amounting to three hundred pounds annually, & she had the place cultivated. At her death it would revert to two of her husband's nephews, one of whom had brought her there, & apparently he welcomed this means of getting rid of her. He feigned urging her to return with him, but felt sure that she had too much attachment for the Religion to be guilty of such cowardness. She, wishing to go to England or Holland, & having heard that I was from Dauphiné & had the same plan, requested me, through some Languedoc merchants, to take her under my care during the voyage, & to arrange about her passage money. The day preceding our departure the English merchants came to visit us & brought bad news for this poor woman. They said that a young Lord, belonging to one of the first families of England, who had returned several days before from Rome, where he had changed his Religion, had taken a notion to sail on the vessel that was to carry us, & as he was an utter debauchee, they would not advise the lady to embark with him, unless I should have the kindness to pretend I was her husband. She was over forty-five years old, but as he often took more wine than he could carry, these Gentlemen feared he might insult her. I promised them & her all that they wished, & consequently there was no question of passage money. She sailed as I did, that is, for nothing.

The decision of this Lord was doubly inconvenient, for we had to give up to him and his governor the room meant for us, & were confined to the stock-room for arms & powder, with his servants. We were somewhat relieved to find them respectable people. He had an English man-servant who spoke good French, a lackey from Montpellier & of the Religion, a very good boy, & a Neapolitan trumpeter, a very honest man. He had married in Marseilles, & he was so moved to compassion at seeing us escape in this fashion that, noticing I had not purchased a bed for my servant, & that he slept upon my coat, when he left he gave us his own, which had cost him a pistole at Leghorn.

Monsieur Christophle Parker, one of the English merchants, knowing at what hour we were to go aboard, was waiting for us on shore, & had ordered put in the boat carrying us to the vessel, a case of forty bottles of Florence Muscat wine, of which he made me a present, & he gave me a letter of introduction to a rich London merchant named Monsieur Jean Brokin, & so as the distance from my native land increased, so did God grant me friends & consolations, according to the promises He made us in His Gospel.

THIRD VOYAGE

VOYAGE TO SPAIN

WE left Leghorn on the 6th of February & sailed without mishap for twelve or fifteen days, & after sighting the island of Majorca coasted along the Kingdom of Catalonia. The sea having great depth along the Spanish coast, the winds were very favorable, & we kept so close to the shore that we could see this beautiful land as well as though we had been ashore, & could even easily discern people walking. In the same way we coasted along the Kingdoms of Valencia, Murcia, Leon, Aragon, & landed in the Kingdom of Granada, at the port of Malaga, where we stopped three days. There I met three Gascons, one of whom owned an inn where I lodged. The city is large, well fortified on the seaward-side because of the neighboring Moors. It has a fine Castle & strong Citadel, where the King of Spain keeps horse & foot garrison; the cavalry are well mounted but wretchedly accoutred. The streets are so narrow that carriages can be ridden only in the suburbs; the ladies, when they go forth, wear a long black silk mantle that covers them from head to heels & leaves but one opening, no larger than a teston, for the left eye. Thus no part of the body can be seen but this one eye. The Nobility also are black garbed; they always wear a cloak, & carry long swords, their hats have brims almost two feet wide, lined with black taffeta & turned up on both sides. They are very courteous to strangers, & as sometimes there is mire where the pavement is broken up & it is necessary to cross it on stones, they stand aside, hat in hand, & beckon one to go first; the common people, on the contrary, are rude & boorish, & far from aiding would, if they dared, push you in. There is nothing worthy of interest but the Church, renowned as the largest & most beautiful in all Spain; but as I am not overfond of visiting Churches, although I did visit this one, I found something which pleased me more, for Malaga is the city that produces the delicious white & claret Spanish wine so famous throughout Europe, & even in America, & so very cheap that all of us, down to the last sailor, laid in some of it. After getting our water-supply we set sail. We had gone hardly ten or twelve leagues along the Andalusian coast when we ran upon four vessels from London, & after exchanging salutes one of the shipmasters came aboard & warned us against crossing the Straits alone, as twenty-two frigates of the Turkish corsairs had been sighted thereabout. It was necessary to stop somewhere, & the wind having shifted against us, we could not

[75]

reach the Pillars of Hercules, four or five leagues away, so were forced to put in, in the neighborhood of Tangiers, in Africa, where we remained two or three days, awaiting an escort. We were joined only by an English tartan loaded with lemons out of Naples, with a crew of six or seven men, but a fair wind blowing for the Straits, we put off & this boat almost caused our destruction, as I shall subsequently relate.

FOURTH VOYAGE

VOYAGE TO ENGLAND

HARDLY had we crossed the Straits than the watch aloft the main-mast called out he saw two vessels directly in our course, & a moment later that he could see two others, somewhat in the distance. The captain immediately ordered the boat to keep close by us, sent the pennon of a man-of-war up the main-mast, & had our thirty guns loaded. The English lord's trumpeter also climbed above the stern & sounded the charge, which went far to impress the pirates that we were indeed a man-of-war. All was made ready for a fight, & we bore straight upon them. When they saw us approaching, they hoisted the French banner, but this did not deceive us into believing they were not corsairs. We had forty sailors, the captain, the purser, the surgeon & three pilots, but as to soldiers, there were only this lord, his governor, who was a captain of infantry, myself, his servants & my own. There was also another English passenger, but he went to hide in the hold, & thereafter the lord, who had always allowed him to take his meals with his servants because he was a papist, refused ever to see him again. The boldness of our captain, a very good man, astonished the pirates, & when we were within shooting range & they did not fire, he sailed closer, until within earshot, to ask whether they were French; they replied they were not, that they were Turks. He demanded their reason for flying a white flag, & they did not know what to answer, but inquired the name of his ship. He named one of the finest men-of-war of the king of England, & we sailed past, but two weeks later we heard they had captured four Flemish vessels. Our own ship would surely have been well worth the taking, for she carried more than five hundred thousand pounds' worth of merchandise. We saw no more of the pirates, but as we sailed oceanward we had our share of tempests & adverse winds, it being the end of February, which, with the month of March, is the stormiest of the year, & consequently the most dangerous to navigation.

The boat that followed us was so slow that we could set but two sails, & even then went faster than she did with all of hers, & she delayed us eight or nine days at least. We sailed for five weeks after leaving the Straits, until one day our Pilot thought that on the morrow we would sight the first English land, but at midnight such a furious tempest arose that for eight days we saw neither sun nor stars, & no observations could be taken. We were thrown this way & that on the vessel, with such violence that it was impossible to sleep during this time, & we could hardly eat. The boat following lost us, but fortunately sailed between the Scilly Islands[1] & the mainland, a passage where large vessels cannot navigate without danger, because of the reefs, & she reported the news of our loss. On the 8th day the masts were lowered, all the sails furled, & we abandoned ourselves unto God's mercy, the ship being out of control; the tempest grew mightier in leaving us, & it was more terrible in our sleeping quarters than in any other part of the ship, for the arms & cannon-balls were kept there, & the cases containing them were broken open by the violence of the tempest, so that they rolled from side to side making a frightful din, with none to stop them, as all were busy elsewhere. Towards midnight, after these nine days, God had compassion upon us & we made out a few stars, & the next day saw the sun; about noon the pilots discovered we had been thrown on the coast of Ireland, although we saw no land; it was a very dangerous place, because of the rocks, which luckily we escaped, & God giving us fair winds after the storm, six days later we reached Gravesin [Gravesend], seven leagues from London. It is there that the large ships unload half their cargo before proceeding farther. This was the last of March, 1686, & had we not been delayed by that boat, we would have made this port ahead of the great storm.

---

[1]Durand wrote "île de cely" for Scilly Islands, and further on "*Gravesin*" for Gravesend.

Meanwhile the poor lady I had taken under my protection at Leghorn was so afraid of the sea, or of what she had been told of the English lord, whom she saw or heard carousing as was his wont, that she fell ill of a tertian fever the day after we sailed, & the fierce storm we went through changed it into a double tertian, with such weakness that she was unable to leave her bed, & I wondered how I should get her off the ship. She was thought to be my wife & I did not contradict this, as it assuredly spared her a good deal of annoyance that she would otherwise have suffered from the lord, ill as she was. He entered her room but once, with shameful talk; his trumpeter immediately called the captain, who came down, & requested him to go away. His servants were all such good people that whenever they saw him in that state heading for our room they called the captain, & thus prevented him from entering, except that one time. When sober he was glad enough to converse with me, but as his talk was mostly about religion, & he seemed bigoted for the one he had just embraced, I often avoided him, for I could not always have refrained from saying what would have offended him, & I did not wish any trouble in a country where we were given so safe a re-treat. He left us at Gravesin. I realized that the poor lady was too weak to wait on the shore of the Thames until I could find a room, so I left my servant to look after her, & also my boy, who had been taken sick as she had, & I went to London, by the grace of God in such good health that although I had never been upon the sea before embarking at Marseilles, I had not been at all seasick. At the first houses we came to, unacquainted as I was of the size of the city, I asked to be landed, & looked for a room to rent, but no one understood me. I roamed around for some time until, by signs and otherwise, I made a man understand that I wished him to take me where there were Frenchmen, in consideration for which I promised to pay him a good deal of money, which I showed him. He finally brought me to the Exchange, & left me in the hands of a Frenchman. To move this man to compassion, I related all that had happened to me. He said he was not of the Religion, but nevertheless for me not to worry, as although he lived a league & a half away, he would not leave me until I had found lodgings. We unsuccessfully sought a room in this quarter, but finding none, I bethought myself of the letter Mr. Christophle Parker had given me at Leghorn. We inquired so carefully for the house of Mr. Brokin that the street was pointed out, & we walked & had no difficulty in locating the house. He was not home, so I begged Madame Brokin to open the letter, & help me find a room. She immediately sent her housekeeper to rent one for me opposite her house, & she had us given food & drink, a timely blessing, for it was six o'clock in the evening & I had eaten nothing & was worn out with fatigue from walking so long on the London pavements, the worst I have ever seen.

The next day, which was Saturday, I returned early to Gravesin, to convey my patients as best I could. The Guards at Dover allowed me to take only the beds from my belongings, & when we returned, my servant & the boatman had to carry the poor sick woman up to the room & I had to carry my boy most of the time, but fortunately it was close to the river. The next day being Sunday, I inquired so diligently & tramped so much from early morning that, after being taken to several English Churches, I was finally taken to the French Temple of London,[1] where I arrived in good time before the beginning of the first sermon. And it was there, with a joy beyond my power to express, at having retrieved this precious light of the Gospel carried out of our kingdom, that I rendered my humble thanks to the Eternal for my escape from Babylon, & my happy arrival in these fortunate countries where truth can be preached without fear or hindrance.

---

[1]At the end of the seventeenth century there were no less than thirty-five French churches in London or its vicinity. Eleven of them were in Spitalfields, which had become the favorite residence of the refugees. The oldest church was on Threadneedle Street, and is called by Smiles "the cathedral church of the Huguenots." There the Huguenots generally repaired on arriving. Samuel Smiles, *The Huguenots, their Settlements, Churches, and Industries in England and Ireland*, New York (1868), p. 270.

FIFTH VOYAGE

THE JOURNEY TO LONDON

WHEN I was back in our lodgings, the poor lady thanked me again for the care I had taken of her person & honor, & not only begged me not to abandon her, ill as she was, but also not to enlighten people that she was not my wife, so that I might obtain assistance for her should her illness linger, for she had but little money left; & also in order that they might not entertain a wrong opinion of her good character for having taken such a long voyage with strangers; for if God gave back her health so she could move about, she would doubtless find acquaintances from Languedoc who would easily dispel any evil suspicions regarding her virtue. I replied that I had already intended to do so, even without her request, & that she should now think of remedies to restore her health; that God in his mercy had permitted me to leave from home with sufficient means because I had been preparing for it a long time, seeing the manner in which we were treated, although I never thought it would go to such extremes; I had hardly doubted they would deprive us of the free exercise of our Religion, but supposed that this would be the extent of our persecution. This having come to pass, I was ready to go even to the end of the world to seek the predication of truth & for this I would use up even to my last penny rather than submit. So I had both attended to, & indeed both began to recover a little. The lady's fever went back to tertian, & my boy's diminished, but they were so weak that it was several days before they could get up & remain seated by their beds. As we were in urgent need of our clothing & I knew not whom to approach, the following Wednesday I went to hear the sermon & thence to the Consistory, where I begged the gentlemen to have my clothes restored to me, being in great need of them because I had two patients. They requested Monsieur Herman Olmyus, a very honest English merchant, to help me, which he did most generously, for he was kind & charitable, not only in this occurrence, but on several other occasions. He spoke good French, & was so obliging that, as I needed him daily because of the language, he left everything to aid me, although he had a great deal of business, nor did he ever let me leave his house without giving me a drink of Spanish wine.

Meanwhile Monsieur Brokin returned from the country & straightway sent for me. He offered to serve me in many ways & often had me eat at his house; so often indeed that had I so desired, I could have eaten there every day. Nay, more, he had meat reserved for my patients & sent them both meat & broth.

When I saw their condition had begun to improve I was a little freer to see the city. I went to call upon Monsieur de Bourdieu,[1] the famous pastor of Montpellier, & to pay him the respects of Messieurs Mire, merchants at Marseilles, who had taken refuge at Leghorn two days before the advent of the Dragoons, & had paid a hundred pistoles to the Master of an English vessel to transport them. He was Pastor, with his son, of a Church at Savoy. He greeted me warmly & put himself at my service.

Savoy is the largest suburb of London. There the King, the Dowager Queen, & most of the Court's great lords have their dwellings. There also are two French Churches, with another in the city; most of the French live at Savoy, or in Despedlefil [Spitalfields], a suburb on the other side, as rents are cheaper than in London.[2]

---

[1]Isaac du Bourdieu, Protestant minister of a noble family of Bearn, fled to London and preached until he reached the age of 95. His son, Jean-Armand, had been a minister at Montpellier and shortly before the Revocation arrived in London with a group of refugees. He became chaplain of the Schomberg family and was at the battle of Boyne. Among the refugees he was outstanding because of his charity, his zeal and his violent invectives against the French "Pharaoh."

[2]An Episcopal Church had been opened by the French refugees in the suburb of Savoy as early as 1641. There Abbadie, Saurin, and du Bourdieu preached. Without reluctance, the French Huguenots joined the English Episcopal Church in England, as well as in the colonies. It seems that this was a way for them to identify themselves with the inhabitants of their new country.

England is a fine country, very rich & with an abundance of all kinds of grain, vegetables, & especially pastures; they raise quantities of cattle, & the only fault to be found with butcher's meat is that it is too fat. Their estates are tithable only for the maintenance of bishops & ministers; merchandise & tin-mines are taxed, & this together with their great commerce makes England the wealthiest country in Europe: consequently beggars are rarely seen upon the streets or at church doors. But what undoubtedly contributes to the fertility of the soil is that the rain falls almost daily during winter & spring; or there rises a kind of draggling fog so thick that there is rarely a clear, fair day; thus the air is damp & heavy & those unaccustomed to it suffer from inflammation of the lungs. As for myself, I was far from feeling as well as I had when on the sea. It happened that in France I had perused pamphlets concerning Carolina, & during our voyage had often discussed them with the lady.[1] I made careful inquiry in order to ascertain whether they told the truth. She was from the country & liked the city no more than I; she understood thoroughly the management of a farm, & told me that on her own estate she had very successfully raised a quantity of silkworms; that she left no regrets in France, & if I went & would take her along, since there were plenty of mulberry trees, she would place in my care the little money she had

[1]On emigration propaganda see *Introduction,* p. 39.

left;[1] that she had clothes & linen enough to last her for life, also some furniture, & that she would take charge of my household & spend the rest of her days with me. I acknowledge that I came to London prejudiced in favor of this country, & that my delight was complete upon receiving confirmation of the truth of the pamphlets & by this woman's decision.

However, I did not wish to undertake such a long journey without consulting my friends, so I went to visit Monsieur de Bourdieu, who had shown me such kindness, to discuss it with him. He said sincerely that he would not advise my going to that country, but that he would exert himself in my behalf to procure me an honest living for two or three years, then, as we were from neighboring provinces, we should return to France: for he was seventy years old, & did not intend to die before he had preached again at Montpellier. I was shaken in my decision, but upon leaving his house I met a man of my acquaintance who told me that Monsieur Pyoset, Pastor of the Church of London,[2]

---

[1] In the seventeenth and eighteenth century many attempts were made to introduce the silk industry into Virginia and the Carolinas (P. A. Bruce, *Economic History of Virginia*, I, p. 366 *et seq.*) In the middle of the seventeenth century, Governor Bruce had even thought of bringing colonists from Italy and Provence for that purpose (*Id.*, p. 400), and later Jefferson considered reviving the experiment. The colonists, however, preferred to cultivate tobacco, and silk was never produced in Virginia in commercial quantities.

[2] Charles Pyozet, formerly minister at Le Mans, was authorized July 26, 1682, to remain in England, and in March, 1685, received

who had also offered me his services, had received a letter from a merchant of his home town who had gone to that country a short while before. I went to see him again, & he said that he had received only good reports about it, & that he advised me to go, warning me, however, to be careful in my choice of a ship-master, for the writer of the letter told of having been badly treated by the captain of the vessel on which he had taken passage. Therefore I followed the last advice, for God had intended me to suffer.

As I was absolutely set upon taking this voyage, I started buying furniture, iron tools for work, & iron fittings to build a house; but money has no handle by which to keep it back, & no sooner had I bought one thing than someone came to tell me I would need also this & that, & that those who had gone before me had taken it along; so little by little I went on spending much money, & although I had not been more than five or six weeks in London, I had already paid either for the care of my patients or for the things I have just mentioned, more than forty Louis d'or.

When I saw my money disappear so rapidly, & being urged by the lady, whom someone had convinced that she might recover on the sea, as so many others had

his denization. He was an influential member of the "Refuge of London," and from 1683 until 1698, a syndic of the French Church of Threadneedle Street. I am indebted to Professor Ascoli, of the Sorbonne, for this information.

done, I went to speak with the captain of a vessel that was to sail the following Friday, this being Monday. They charge twenty écus a head for this voyage, in consideration of which you are stowed between decks, three in a bed, & once a day are fed pea soup, salt-beef three days a week & the remaining four days the most unsavoury codfish that can be found, at least this was how we were treated by him with whom we sailed.[1] To procure what they call the large room, with two uncomfortable beds, one for my patients, & a corner where I could place my small mattress, I had to give thirty shillings more, with nothing but water to drink. And I who detest fish, was forced to make other arrangements for food & drink. I agreed, however, to go with him & again saw myself put to an expense of thirty pistoles & at that had to live very poorly.

---

[1]P. A. Bruce (*Economic History of Virginia*, I, p. 630) indicates that the passage price for the lowest class was about £5.10. This was exactly what Durand had to pay. Durand, however, gives details regarding the accommodations and fare which are not to be found elsewhere. For information concerning the stores, and particularly the tools and nails, taken along by the immigrants, see also Bruce, *Ibid*, II, p. 146.

SIXTH VOYAGE

VOYAGE TO CAROLINA IN THE WEST INDIES

I WENT to Gravesend to meet our ship & was much surprised to find there were no French people aboard, although the Master had told me he was carrying six, & that some of them could speak English. He informed me, for I still had my interpreter, that in truth six were to sail with him but, hearing of a collection to be taken up, they had remained in the hope of getting some money.[1] I had to accept the situation; I had paid him. We sailed to Dyel [Deal], where we dropped anchor & were joined by three or four English merchants, some of whom had their wives & children, & Monsieur Ysné,[2] a man 32 or 33 years old, of very handsome appearance & good mind, who spoke very good French.

---

[1] This was the Royal Bounty, a fund established in 1681, to assist the refugees. New collections had recently been ordered, beginning April 23, 1686.

[2] This very curious character, whose name was really Parker, and who was related to the Disney or d'Isney family, will reappear later.

He told me that he was the factor of rich London merchants who were sending him over with merchandise, in order to try to establish trade with that country. Not only was he a great comfort because he spoke French, but, in addition, he proved to be the most honest & the most obliging man I have ever met. When all the passengers that were to take ship were aboard, we put off, but after going thirty or forty leagues were twice forced to return to Dyel [Deal]; we started once more, & after getting as far as the Isle of Wicht [Wight], then had to put back to Rye. Thus for four weeks we sailed from one port to the other, always with contrary winds from the west, until finally we reached Falmouth, the last English port. The captain proved to be such an honest man that when it was necessary for me to go ashore to get something for my patients, he even refused to let me use his boat, & I had to hire at great expense the boatmen who came upon the ship selling beer & tobacco; & his sailors, who were no better than he, sometimes returned with an empty boat, in which they refused to take me.

Meanwhile the lady was sick again with a double tertian fever, & my boy was noticeably falling away. So when I had someone inquire of the master whether he expected to stay some time in this port, he let me know that if the wind did not shift for a month, or even two, he would not leave, & that vessels had been weatherbound there as long as that. Thereupon I went to the city with Monsieur Ysné, who declared he would not leave me, & we found a French surgeon, four years in that place. I requested him to engage a room where my patients could rest a few days. He rented one for 30 sous a week, & having hired a boat, I asked him to send it over early the next morning, & had them carried to it. But towards noon, as we were told that the wind had shifted a little to the south, I had them ready, dressed, on their beds, & about six o'clock went in town to find the captain, to ask whether he intended sailing that day. He said he did not, but that I could put my patients to bed, & if the next day the wind were fair, he would send his boat at dawn for us. Monsieur Ysné, who was along, told me in French he was surprised to find such decency in the brute & that he would not have believed him capable of it. Consequently I had them go to bed & he went back to the ship. When it was getting dark, I saw four sailors enter the room, bringing with them the French surgeon as interpreter to tell me from their barbarous master that we must go aboard at once, & that they had brought the boat, otherwise, he would sail with my belongings. This cruelty drove me to despair; however, being accustomed & inured to all sorts of unpleasant predicaments, I decided immediately & informed the lady that unless God favored us with contrary winds enabling her & my boy to remain a few days in order to regain some strength, she would be in no shape to stand the sea, & that we should not court death to gain earthly goods; that I was ready to sacrifice everything to serve her & we must trust the future to Providence, so she should stay in bed while I went to the ship to have our belongings unloaded. But far from listening to reason, this poor woman threw herself out of bed & dressed as quickly as her weakness would permit.

So we went aboard the ship, at least half a league from the city. Owing to the night dew or to fatigue, her fever became chronic, & although the wind was fair, we did not sail until late the next day. The honest captain, seeing me a stranger & friendless, had thought through this means to gain possession of my effects on his vessel; for had I not come aboard, as he expected me to do, he would surely have left that same night, & he could have justified himself, in case of blame, by saying that he had sent for me & I refused to come.

We were about sixty on board, all told. There were two merchants with their wives & children, besides six others, including Mr. Isné, whom we believed to be a merchant also, all of them very honest people. In addition, the Captain had brought along to be sold, twelve prostitutes & fifteen of the boldest & most insolent young scoundrels in all England.[1]

---

[1] On the manner in which these "servants" were recruited one may consult P. A. Bruce, *Economic History of Virginia,* I, p. 612 *et seq.* Sometimes perfectly honorable young men were kidnapped and sequestered for months before being "sold" to a shipmaster. Others were glad to seize this opportunity to escape from justice. Besides

We left Falmous [Falmouth] accompanied by a vessel bound for Barbados, & had so fair a wind during the first week that it was said, should it continue, we would arrive within a month. But after eight or nine days, our conductor, who was not only brutal but ignorant of the art of navigation as well, having never before been in command of a ship, decided to part company with the other vessel, giving as his reasons that we were traveling ahead of summer, & that he was going to steer northward, so that later a north wind would put us back on our latitude; our real course, however, lay two-thirds of the way with this other vessel, which did, indeed, one month after leaving us, reach Barbados, which is almost as far as Carolina, as we learned long after sailing.

I had become very friendly with Monsieur Isné, & in fact he hardly talked with anyone but me. His behaviour was so civil & noble that he easily won my esteem & not entirely against my will I felt compelled to be more courteous with him than with the others, although I supposed them to be of the same station; so that when those shameless creatures kept singing & dancing above my patients, I often requested him to complain to the captain. He not only complied, but

these unscrupulous recruiting agents there were also duly accredited "agencies" for the prospective colonists. See James Curtis Ballagh, *White Servitude in the Colony of Virginia,* Johns Hopkins University Studies in Historical and Political Science, 13th series, Vols. VI-VII. Baltimore, 1895.

strove to prevent them, as much as he could, whereas the brute only laughed. This filled me with such a dislike for these creatures that, had I been on a French vessel, I believe I would have thrown a few of them into the ocean.

Certainly their insolence wrought a change in my nature, for my acquaintances would no doubt impute to me, as my greatest failing, an exaggerated love of the fair sex, & to tell the truth I must admit that in my youth there was no injustice in this accusation. Not that I was ever coarse or low enough to feel an affection for prostitutes, but I am obliged to confess that I did not abhor their debauchery as I should have. Thus was I like a certain stoic philosopher who, having unconsciously become avaricious, one day saw displayed in a triumph in ancient Rome all the rich spoils from the East, & overcame his passion at the sight of so much treasure. In the same way, as I slept but little, being sunk in gloom and sorrow, & got up at all hours of the night, I saw those wenches behave so shockingly with the sailors & others, in addition to the distress caused by their songs & dances, that it awakened within me so intense a hatred of such persons that I shall never overcome it. I cannot truthfully say, however, that as my loathing for this sort of thing grew, the respect & veneration I have always felt for those who professed themselves modest & virtuous has proportionately increased.

Meanwhile we were sailing so straight north, the

south wind always blowing, that we found ourselves several degrees above New England, where we met enormous whales, & were forced to come back along the coast, fifty leagues from the land, taking all the month of July to sail along New England, New York, Pennsylvania, & Virginia, & until we reached the latitude of Virginia & Maryland we had to wear hose & clothing usually worn in mid-winter.

It was in the tenth week after our departure from London that God was pleased to call the poor lady. I sincerely regretted her, for she was a woman of high virtue & would have helped me greatly in getting established. I would have regretted her still more, however, had she lived sometime longer, for we began to have a shortage of supplies; but at least I still had some of the wine & all the provisions I had brought along. I served her the best I could. I had a servant, a good man, who had come with me from France, & he also served her kindly & constantly; then, as if I had not already had enough to crush me, three days later God took my boy. So much loss reduced me to a pitiable state & I prayed God zealously & fervently, to put an end to all this grief & suffering by a quick death, but my time had not yet come. Monsieur Isné sympathized with me in my despair & comforted me as much as possible. Certainly my grief was incomparably greater than if all this had happened in England, for I would not then have hesitated to follow the advice of Monsieur de Bourdieu.

And now I thought of myself in a country where, should my servant leave me, I would be helpless & alone. I was not meant for work, but I had no other means of livelihood; my despondency caused my mind to dwell upon these dark thoughts.[1] But as God never sends hard trials upon us without giving us the means of overcoming them, & patience to bear them, I began to reflect that Providence having so liberally provided me with friends & other things since my departure from France, surely would not abandon me in America; thus I began to be comforted & to recover some serenity.

At last on the first of August, when our numskull of a captain thought we were within twenty-four leagues of Carolina, we came upon a vessel out from Barbados, & were very glad to speak with them. The skiff was lowered & the master of that ship came to ours & told us we had gone so far from the course that we were still two hundred leagues from Charleston. The Merchants all told him they were going to settle in that country, described in some pamphlets they had with them as the most beautiful & the most fertile of all America, & many persons in London had assured them that this was true. The captain answered that two years previously he had landed there thirty-two people from Plymouth,

---

[1] The sufferings of the immigrants during the sea voyage are hardly believable. In 1680, Lord Culpeper wrote that, "death, scurvy and calenture" prevailed on the passenger ships accompanying him. P. A. Bruce, *Economic History,* I, pp. 136–139.

all of them in vigorous health, but that eleven months later, when he returned, only two were alive, & that there was not an acre of good soil in all south Carolina. One of our own sailors added he had been there in July the year before, & half of Charleston had either left or were dead.[1]

This information astonished the merchants, & upon learning that his vessel was carrying negroes & sugar to be sold in Maryland, where she would take on a cargo of tobacco, they struck a bargain with him to drop them off at the first land he should pass in Virginia. So as we lay becalmed for two days, they had all their merchandise transferred to the other ship, & left us. Monsieur Isné was one of them. He did his best to persuade me to go along, but I told him that I had not heard there were any Frenchmen in Virginia, so I could not be otherwise than badly off there, & although I was loath to take leave of him, I must submit to fate, having gone so far. It was the master of this ship who said that the vessel leaving Falmouth with us arrived at Barbados one month after we parted company. I remained, as did two merchants & one carpenter; & now our wretchedness increased a great deal. As we approached the latitude of Carolina we began to feel the heat of its climate. Shortly before, a severe storm had broken the hoops of the only barrel of salt pork left us. The salt water

[1]See the diary of Judith Guiton in Baird, French edition, p. 363, and G. Chinard, *Les Réfugiés Huguenots*, p. 202 *et seq.*

leaked out & the meat spoiled, so we could not eat it. All on board were rationed to three pounds of mouldy biscuit a week & a pitcher of water a day. Although I had been very sparing of my wine, I had finished it a week or ten days before. But all this was as nothing compared to the grief I suffered. After Monsieur Isné left it awakened anew, stronger than ever; & I can say that because of it hunger, & thirst & all other miseries mattered little to me.

Or if they did affect me, it was rather for my servant's sufferings than for my own. And yet of all on board, it was I who endured most, for they at least had some bad salt cod to eat, & as we neared land the sailors caught almost as much fresh fish as was needed. But for myself, I have such a dislike for all sorts of fish that I could never taste it. It is true that when I left my country to follow truth, I was ready to suffer trials, if God so willed it, but I confess that this sort of affliction overwhelmed me, for I had not expected it.

Contrary west winds so hindered our progress that we reached the Gulf of Florida only on the tenth of September. Such a gale was blowing that we made small headway, but finally one morning we saw land, for which we were well pleased, & began preparations for sleeping at Charleston. There must be great quantities of birds in that country, for a great multitude of all sizes covered our masts. But about noon, with no increase of wind, the waters of the gulf grew so rough that our prow was smashed to pieces, & the mast above snapped at its base. This fell against the main-mast & broke two shafts, but our ship was so strong, as she had been built but four years back, that she held up miraculously, otherwise we would all have been lost. We were thrown back on the open sea, & a jury-mast was rigged up in some way to set one sail, but not daring to attempt this passage again, we sailed towards Virginia, where, God having sent us a fair wind, although we had scarcely any sails, we arrived seven or eight days later. During this time three or four people died for want of water, although there was still plenty, but this inhuman master would allow them to be given only their ration. We dropped anchor in the North river, half a league from shore.[1] The inhabitants of the place came to visit us, among them being a Frenchman who had bought off his indenture, & wishing to go ashore with him, I changed my clothes all covered with pitch & tar for a suit I had not worn since Marseilles. I had to draw in the belt to my breeches sixteen inches.

---

[1]North River, Mobjack Bay.

A BRIEF DESCRIPTION OF AMERICA
WITH A LONGER ONE OF
VIRGINIA & MARYLAND

I LANDED with great joy, on the 22nd of September, 1686, after being nineteen weeks at sea. From the time we reached the Indies, I wrote down every week all I had seen, & what I now give is practically the last thing I recorded. But for a better understanding of the voyages I am about to describe, I have thought fit to remove it from its place & use it here.

The King of England possesses in America six colonies on the mainland & three beautiful islands; that is to say, New England, New York, Pennsylvania, Maryland, Virginia & Carolina, & for islands, the Bermudas, Barbados, & Jamaica.

Pennsylvania, New England, New York, are in the 40°, 41°, 42°, 43° degrees. A great variety of grain is grown there, as in England; it is also a land of fertile pastures for the raising of cattle, or at least so they told me, for what I saw from the sea when I was opposite their shores was colder than England. They produce iron, hemp, flax, pitch & tar. There is a fine city called Baston,[1] whose inhabitants trade with the islands. Wheat is shipped by them, & when they run short, it is purchased in Virginia & reshipped. They exchange it for sugar & rhum, a kind of brandy made from the dregs of sugar, cotton, & spices, not only for themselves, but for Virginia & Maryland, as the inhabitants of these two colonies never leave their country.

To the north of New England lies New France or Canada. It is a land so cold that only oats & a few vegetables grow there. The Indians of New England bring them corn in trade for skins of wild animals. The King of France provides them with some, also.

Carolina is divided into two parts, called South & North. In the south is Charleston, with about two hundred houses. All the French who have gone over have settled in the south. In any of the American possessions of the King of England each foreigner wishing to settle is given fifty acres of land. In Carolina one must pay a sol a year for every acre,[2] but in Virginia one pays the King only two shillings for one hundred acres, as it is held direct from him, there being no private owners.

---

[1]Boston; a frequent spelling with French travellers and cartographers in the seventeenth and eighteenth centuries, and probably an attempt to reproduce phonetically the pronunciation still current in New England.

[2]On conditions offered to the refugees in Carolina see Arthur Henry Hirsch, *The Huguenots of Colonial South Carolina,* Ch. VIII, "The Economic Success of the Huguenots." One may believe that Mr. Hirsch has painted too rosy a picture, and neglected the sufferings and failures of the immigrants.

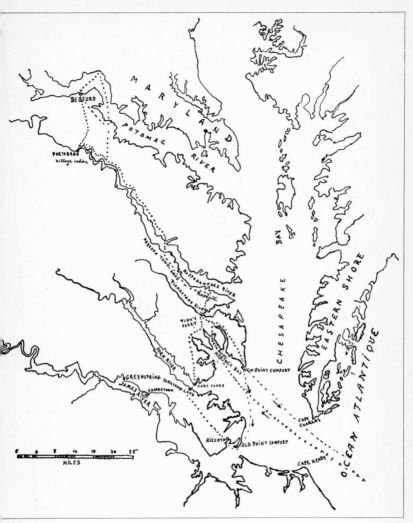

Plate III.   VIRGINIA IN 1686

There are beautiful cedars, much larger & straighter than those of Virginia, walnut-trees, a great number of mulberry, fig, peach, cherry & apple trees, but no olive, orange, or lemon trees, wild vines, or cotton, as claimed by the pamphlets. They have only hand-mills & pestles for grinding their corn, & will have trouble in building water-mills, for the country is too flat & too wooded for wind-mills. I think the soil is as rich as in the provinces along the Gemerive [James River], in southern Virginia, & Indian corn grows there as in other parts of America. Wheat grows with difficulty, & is not good, being more than half husk. I met a man worthy of credence, who had come thence. He was from New York, & told me that had he wished to eat wheat-bread it would have cost him six sols a pound, & mutton, 7 sols, but that for wine the French had sent over cuts of Madeira vines from which a fair harvest of good quality had already been reaped by some. There are many oxen, cows & pigs, few or hardly any sheep, quantities of fowl & game. It is un-healthy for Frenchmen, which does not surprise me, for the southern provinces of Virginia four degrees further north are also very unhealthy. This is what I heard of these countries from persons of honor, who may be be-lieved. All of these colonies adjoin on the west, but there are as yet no roads for travelling from one to the other. I have seen pamphlets in which it was also said that in these countries winter began when it was spring in Europe, but this is not true either; December, January & February are their winter months. I did remark something differing from our climate; I found that in December the days are longer & the sun follows a higher course, but none could give me an explanation for it. It happened that on the nineteenth of the same month, when I went to pay my respects to the Governor of Virginia, I was in a room where a very accurate clock struck five, & observed that the sun was still shining against the windows. This caused me, as soon as I reached my chamber, to borrow a water-clock, & on the 22nd, the day reckoned by pilots as the shortest of the year, as soon as it was light enough to read, I set it, & being careful to turn it promptly every hour, counted eleven hours of daylight, & thus ascertained that in these countries the days decrease but one hour & consequently increase the same.

I went fifty leagues into the country & from there could see high mountains, like the Alps, covered with eternal snows.[1] Beyond, in South America, are Peru, where rich gold mines may be found, Brazil, & all the beautiful islands that the Spaniards & Portuguese possess. From thence the lovely rivers watering Virginia flow.

---

[1] If one refers to the itinerary of Durand, it will be readily seen that, although he has travelled more than fifty leagues, he has, contrary to his assertion, never been very far into the country. The hills he was able to distinguish had nothing in common with the Alps, and of course were not covered with "eternal snows."

Bermuda, Barbados & Jamaica are very good & fine countries. Much sugar is produced in the first two, & they grow some wheat, but Jamaica does not. There orange & lemon trees grow wild, & the climate of the country suits negroes so well that they are another large source of revenue. Some of the inhabitants will have five hundred males & females, multiplying very fast, & as soon as their children are twelve or thirteen years old they are sold to the people on the mainland, & this brings them great wealth. They also have spices, cotton & indigo.

Maryland was discovered before Virginia, in the reign of Queen Mary. At first both Catholics & Protestants settled here, & they have always intermingled. There are churches & temples, priests & ministers, but they live in close union & harmony.

Virginia was discovered sometime later, under Queen Elizabeth, & is called Virginia for this Queen who never married. To approach either of these two colonies, one must pass the "Cap de Bies," two heavily wooded promontories at the south, about a league apart. Ships must sail through this strait, into which sand is frequently washed from the Gulf of Florida, thus making the passage dangerous for large vessels, especially in winter, & there are always some of them wrecked. On the promontory at the left-hand side coming towards the land, are four counties of Virginia separated from the rest by the Gemerive [James River], which empties into the Cape, & they are bordered by Carolina. At the promontory on the right are four other counties, separated from the rest by an arm of the ocean called Bées,[1] which, three leagues up from the mouth, widens to six leagues, & keeps about the same width until it reaches Maryland, where it continues about thirty leagues into this province & then stops. Into this inlet flow four large rivers, which are, beginning with the most northern, the broad Pethomak [Potomac], three leagues wide at its estuary, the Rappahannak [Rappahannock], the York, & the Gemerive [James river].[2] The Rappahannak is the next largest, the York, which is the smallest, is still larger than the Rhone between Baucaire & Tarascon.

Virginia, that is to say the part inhabited by Christians, for the rest, although belonging to it has no name, forms twenty-six counties or provinces, & Maryland has twelve. It is the most beautiful, agreeable & fertile country in all the West Indies. The four great rivers flow through it for over thirty leagues & empty into Bées.

In Virginia the practice of the Protestant religion alone is tolerated. There may be a few Roman Catholics, but they attend Protestant services. Virginia is on

---

[1]The entrance to the Chesapeake Bay, between Cape Charles and Cape Henry.

[2]According to the "Virginian" this curious spelling reproduces approximately a pronunciation still current in Virginia.

the 36th & 37th degrees of latitude, the air is temperate, it is never foggy, the rains that fall in all seasons are as gentle as those of May in France; the snow is never over half a foot deep, & never remains more than three days on the ground. I tarried there until March fifteenth, 1687. I know not what the weather was like in Europe, but in this country I witnessed only three snowfalls: the first, of one inch, the next of two, & the third of half a foot. It lay but three days on the ground, & the inhabitants declared it the most severe winter they had ever seen. When the north wind blows it grows very cold & freezes hard, but when it stops their winters are like our springs in France. I believe I may safely compare the mean temperature to that of Montélimar & St. Paul, Trois Chateaux in Dauphiné. One can judge of it by the fact that wheat is sown at the end of October & beginning of November, & is reaped the fifteenth of June.

There are neither cities nor towns, save one called Jemston [Jamestown],[1] where the Parliament sits. The rest are separate dwellings, each colonist having one on his own plantation. So much tobacco is grown that a hundred & fifty ships might every year be laden with it in Virginia alone. Those buying this tobacco give

---

[1]Phonetic transcription of Jamestown. The town established in 1607 had been destroyed by Richard Lawrence in 1676 during the Bacon rebellion. It was hardly beginning to be rebuilt when Governor Nicholson transferred the court to Williamsburg, which became the capital of Virginia. See Beverley, Book I, Ch. IV.

twenty-four sous a barrel, which brings fifty thousand pounds to the Governor, pays entirely for Parliament, & the five collectors. There are twelve Councilors appointed by the King of England, & one Judge in each county, sitting two days each month. Appeals from his judgments are laid before the Parliament meeting twice a year, during the months of May & October.[1]

The only land taxes are for the ministers & two shillings to the King for each hundred acres. It is true that for the last four or five years there has been a tax for the maintenance of troops. I learned that long ago some sort of treaty was signed with the savages by which they left the sea to the Christians & withdrew far inland, excepting a few who remained. The savages had neither had nor ever heard of small-pox. This sickness, which now & then attacks the Christians of the Indies as well as those of Europe, spread to them, & when they asked what was usually done to cure it, some malicious people told them to find the coldest water they could, & wash all over with it, thus very few of those who had caught it recovered. Whether through hatred because of this, or regret at having left the sea

---

[1]The "Parlement" mentioned here by Durand is not the Assembly, meeting every two years, and of which he does not seem to have even suspected the existence. He probably means the General Court, composed of the Governor and twelve counsellors, which met twice a year, on April 15th and October 15th. Durand's description simplifies in a curious fashion, the system of government and taxes which, in fact, was much more complicated.

& their fishing, they called upon the savages of Canada to help them drive the Christians from Virginia, & promised the plantations as compensation. So they made up a corps, whereupon the Christians being warned, raised troops, & awaiting in battle formation this army of barbarians, defeated them on a plain bordering the Rappahannak river, which was pointed out to me. The native Indians taken were killed, & those from Canada sold as slaves. They were then driven far back into the country & very few remained. The colonels of these troops claimed the plantations of the savages & had them surveyed, so that at the present time there are large tracts of very good land for sale in Virginia.[1]

Since then a few companies of cavalry & infantry have been retained near the frontier provinces to reconnoiter two days a week, although there is nothing to fear, & some small pay is given in tobacco, which is a light charge for this country. Taxes are levied, not according to the amount of land possessed, but according to the number of slaves, thus a man who has two thousand acres of land & only nine slaves pays less than he who has a hundred acres and ten slaves.

The Indies are the refuge of those who, unable to

---

[1] A confirmation of this point will be found in Bruce's *Economic History*, I, p. 188. Durand here sums up in a very unsatisfactory manner more than half a century of struggles against the Indians. It seems certain that the Virginians never formed an alliance with the "Savages of Canada."

earn a livelihood in England, take ship, & are brought over & sold for the price of their passage. They are also the English galleys, for when a person is convicted of a crime not punishable by hanging, he is banished to America to serve his sentence. They are likewise the refuge of bankrupts & the retreat of women who are thieves or lax in matters of chastity & modesty. Therefore it is not surprising that little honesty is to be found among the populace; but this does not apply to the people of quality. They are attracted by the richness of the country, for in England, among the nobility, the estate is given almost entirely to the eldest child, & the younger get only a small legacy, so some of them settle in this new world, where they live in high state on little wealth, & abide in virtue & honor. A difference exists between the slaves that are bought, to wit: a Christian twenty years old or over, cannot be a slave for more than five years, whereas negroes & other unbelievers are slaves all their lives.

There are no lords, but each is sovereign on his own plantation. The gentlemen called Cavaliers are greatly esteemed & respected, & are very courteous & honorable. They hold most of the offices in the country, consisting of twelve seats in Parliament [Court], six collectors, the rank of Colonel in each county, & Captains of each company. It is not necessary to have studied law to be a member of Parliament [Court]. They sit in judgment with girded sword. Monsieur

Wormeley, of whom I shall speak later, is a Councillor, Collector of the Rappahannak river, & Colonel of the same county.

It is a common law country. The laws are so wise that there are almost no law-suits. They never speak of discussion or substitution. When a man squanders his property he squanders his wife's also, & this is fair, for the women are foremost in drinking & smoking. The people spend most of their time visiting each other, whereas we of Europe, with our written law, pass the major part of ours in cares, expense & feuds engendered by the length of our law-suits. The Indians spend theirs eating & drinking together with neither quarrels nor hatreds.

They dress as we do in France. Almost all of their clothes are brought ready-made from England. They do not suffer from bronchitis or gout, & it is because of the climate, for during my stay in London I suffered from a severe cold in my chest, & in this country, by the grace of God, I was completely cured.

The land is so rich & so fertile that when a man has fifty acres of ground, two men-servants, a maid & some cattle, neither he nor his wife do anything but visit among their neighbors. Most of them do not even take the trouble to oversee the work of their slaves, for there is no house, however modest, where there is not what is called a Lieutenant, generally a freedman, under whose commands two servants are placed. This Lieutenant keeps himself, works & makes his two servants work, & receives one-third of the tobacco, grain, & whatever they have planted, & thus the master has only to take his share of the crops. If he commands three or four, his share is proportional. According to law if a slave rebels against his master while he is being whipped, he is condemned to be hanged, & if he rebels against his officer or his Lieutenant, he is condemned to serve two years longer. That is why, when a freedman has served his indenture, he will serve no longer, no matter what salary you offer him, for he can find as many situations of Lieutenant as he wishes.

Money is rarely used, except by the people of quality. They barter with tobacco as though it were specie. With it they buy land, they rent it, they buy cattle, & as they can get anything they need in exchange for this commodity, they become so lazy that they send to England for clothes, linen, hats, women's dresses, shoes, iron tools, nails, & even wooden furniture, although their own wood is very fine to work on, & they have loads of it, such as tables, chairs, bedsteads, chests, wardrobes, in fact everything for house & kitchen. Yet I know that provided with iron & tin they could do without all the rest. Certainly the country should be settled by Europeans, & particularly by the French, whom the King has made very industrious & thrifty because of the heavy taxes with which he has burdened them. In this colony they sell

more than twelve hundred thousand écus' worth of
tobacco, not including what they reserve for barter &
their own use, & this every year, so that if out of that
amount they bought only iron, tin, sugar, spices &
brandy, they could walk upon gold, for in every province there are enough mulberry-trees to produce silk
for their own use, & in those of the south there could
be four times as much as they need.[1] For their clothes
& coverings they would have more than enough wool,
& as fine as that of England; there are quantities of
beavers for making hats, more leather than anything
else for making shoes, & hemp for making linen;
upon my arrival I saw some of it as beautiful & fine as
any in Europe, that they had let spoil after being pulled
up, because not one woman in the whole country knows
how to spin. As for food, it is more abundant than all
else, but to avoid confusion, I shall speak first about
grains, then about animals, & lastly about trees.

---

[1]The same accusation of poor economy is found in Beverley,
Book IV, Ch. 18.

ON THE BEAUTY & FERTILITY OF AMERICA

NORTH America is naturally a very beautiful country, & as for Virginia & Maryland, if you but glance across the plains you will see them covered with lofty trees & lovely orchards of apples, pears, cherries, apricots, figs & peaches. Where there is no timber, there are fine pastures, or lands planted with tobacco, grain, vegetables, & all the necessaries of life. You will see the four great rivers meandering along, & from their tranquil, peaceful course be unable to discern from whence they rise, never overflowing, & never leaving the river-bed. Then if you look to the hills & low mountains, they will not offer you a hideous perspective, as do the mountains of Provence, Genoa & part of Tuscany & part of Spain, covered entirely with stones, rocks & sterile land bare of trees & vegetation, but deep woods, & where they have been cut or uprooted, good pastures & pleasant streams. However, as we poor refugees have greater need for utility than for delight, I shall dwell at greater length upon its fertility.[1]

I have said that the soil in Virginia is very rich both

[1] See Beverley, Book II, Ch. IV, and Book IV, Ch. XXII.

for sowing & planting, but it is not equally good everywhere. In the province of Gloster [Gloucester], where I stayed longest, for it was there I had taken a room when we had landed, there is about half a foot of black earth, in other places a foot, beneath which is sand. In those along the Germinie river [James river], & in southern Virginia, there is less of it, & consequently they yield less; but in that of Rappahannak, what I have seen of the county of Stafford, & particularly on the plantations of Monsieur Wormeley, it is more than a foot, & there are all kinds of soil, as in France, that is to say, heavy black earth, clays, others lighter mixed with small gravel, but black throughout. In the South I observed that the stems of their tobacco were thinner, the stalks of their Indian corn not as high & slenderer, from which I judged that the land was less fertile. They usually plant tobacco, Indian corn, wheat, peas or beans, barley, sweet potatoes, turnips, which grow to a monstrous size & are very good to eat. They make gardens as we do in Europe; hemp & flax grow very high, but as I have already said, they do not know how to prepare it or how to spin. Again the soil is so favorable for fruit-trees that I saw orchards planted, I was told, only ten years before, with larger & better grown trees than our twenty year old ones in Europe.[1]

---

[1] "The Fruit-Trees are wonderfully quick of growth, so that in six or seven years' time from the planting, a man may bring an orchard to bear in great plenty." Beverley, Book IV, Ch. XXII.

In the county of Gloucester wheat generally yields ten to one; Indian corn two hundred to one; the farmers reap only about a bushel of wheat each on their plantations for making pies, because of the great abundance of game & apples which make very good pies also.[1] I asked why they did not grow more of it. They answered it yielded but ten to one, whereas Indian corn gave at least two hundred to one, & they were as healthy on this bread as they would be on that made of wheat. As for barley, they grow little of it, it yields eighteen to one; but they make so much cider, very different from Normandy cider, that if they knew how to manage, they would always have some left at the end of the year. In some places Indian corn yields as much as five hundred to one, which I could not have believed had I not seen it. Bread made of it is as white as paper & agreeable to the taste, but rather heavy on the stomach for those not used to it; nor can the dough be spread to make pies.[2] To mix it they bring water to the oven door & there reknead the dough; when baked it slices like the other kind. Most people grind it in handmills, sift it & use only the choicest for making bread; there remain grains

---

[1] "It is thought too much for the same man, to make the wheat, and grind it, bolt it and bake it himself." Beverley, Book IV, Ch. XXII.

[2] This is probably the "pone" or "bread made of Indian meal," which, according to Beverley, the poorer sort of people preferred to real bread (Book IV, Ch. XVII). Beverley adds that the name comes, not from the Latin *panis*, but from the Indian *oppone*.

like fine rice, which make an excellent but somewhat indigestible soup. With this soup they feed the slaves, & it costs very little to maintain them, particularly the negroes, for in some places they are given bread & meat only on Christmas day. They do not know what it is to plough the land with cattle, but just make holes into which they drop the seeds, although it would be easy to till &, there being no stones, a single horse could be used to plough anywhere.[1] Some possess a hundred cows or oxen & thirty horses for riding only, except on a few plantations too far from the sea & the rivers, where they are used to draw carts. Wood is so handy their slaves always carry it on their shoulders, & I would like to state & aver that were I settled there, provided I had two servants, a plough with two cows & another one with two horses, I could boast of accomplishing more work than anyone in the country with eight strong slaves.

So much timber have they that they build fences all around the land they cultivate. A man with fifty acres of ground, & others in proportion, will leave twenty-five wooded, & of the remaining twenty-five will cultivate half & keep the other as a pasture & paddock for his cattle. Four years later, he transfers his fences to

---

[1]This was the primitive method of cultivation used by the Indians. The stumps of trees would have made regular ploughing very difficult. Bruce states that even at the end of the seventeenth century, ploughs were comparatively rare in Virginia. *Economic History,* I, p. 462.

this untilled half which meanwhile has had a period of rest & fertilization, & every year they put seeds in the ground they till. They sow wheat at the end of October & beginning of November, & corn at the end of April. This is the best grain to harvest, because those needing to can commence using it for bread at the beginning of September & the harvest is not over until the end of November. They only plant about a bushel, as otherwise the field would be too large, for this bushel takes up a lot of ground; they put four seeds close together under a small mound & every four feet apart sow four more. This space is necessary for its growth, because it has big roots, stalks three inches thick & seven or eight feet long. They plant four together so they can hold each other up, against the wind. They also plant two beans of an excellent kind, close to the four grains of corn whose stalks will serve them as poles to climb along. They transplant their tobacco in May, & leave three feet between each plant. Large quantities of it are used in this country, besides what they sell. Everyone smokes while working & idling. I sometimes went to hear the sermon; their churches are in the woods, & when everyone has arrived the minister & all the others smoke before going in. The preaching over, they do the same thing before parting. They have seats for that purpose. It was here I saw that everybody smokes, men, women, girls & boys from the age of seven years.

In the counties of the Rappahannock & Estaford [Stafford], corn yields four or five hundred for one & wheat fifteen or sixteen. What makes me believe it, besides having been told so, is that I saw some not yet gathered which had two or three ears on each cane or stalk; elsewhere I saw but one on each. As to wheat at M. Wormeley's plantations I saw the cows, horses & sheep grazing on it. It was Christmas-time when I was there, & I told him they would spoil it. The servants replied that they left the cattle there until the fifteenth of March, & unless they had it thinned they would gather only straw.

Some people in this country are comfortably housed; the farmers' houses are built entirely of wood, the roofs being made of small boards of chestnut, as are also the walls. Those who have some means, cover them inside with a coating of mortar in which they use oyster-shells for lime; it is as white as snow, so that although they look ugly from the outside, where only the wood can be seen, they are very pleasant inside, with convenient windows & openings. They have started making bricks in quantities, & I have seen several houses where the walls were entirely made of them. Whatever their rank, & I know not why, they build only two rooms with some closets on the ground floor, & two rooms in the attic above; but they build several like this, according to their means. They build also a separate kitchen, a separate house for the Christian

[119]

slaves, one for the negro slaves, & several to dry the tobacco, so that when you come to the home of a person of some means, you think you are entering a fairly large village.[1] There are no stables because they never lock up their cattle. Indeed few of the houses have a lock, for nothing is ever stolen. One can go two hundred leagues with a hatful of pistoles without fear of having a single one stolen. When the women do the washing, if the clothes are not dry that same day, they leave them as long as three days & three nights outside. Robbery is so severely punished that were a man convicted of having stolen a hen, he would be hanged. In the same way all their cattle stay in the woods at night & they fear no thieves but wolves, against which they have faithful dogs; then too, if anyone kills a wolf the State gives him a barrel of tobacco, so for that reason they are very much sought for.

My host had only two young men-servants, no maid; he had bought one of those shameless hussies who came over at the time I did, & she had been ill

---

[1]Beverley, discussing the architecture of the colonists, indicates that they do not "covet" to make their buildings lofty, "having extent enough of ground to build upon; and now and then they are visited by high winds, which would incommode a towring fabrick." He adds that "all their drudgeries of cookery, washing, dairies, etc., are perform'd in offices detacht from the dwelling-houses, which by this means are kept more cool and sweet." Naturally all the buildings were covered with shingles. *History of Virginia*, Book IV, Ch. XVI; see also, P. A. Bruce, *Economic History*, Vol. II, Ch. XII, p. 150 et seq.

Plate IV. A SEVENTEENTH CENTURY HOUSE NEAR WILLIAMSBURG

ever since from work. He gathered ten bushels of wheat, two hundred of corn, having sown a bushel of each; fifteen bushels of beans, a quantity of sweet potatoes, perhaps fifty bushels of turnips had they been measured, & twelve hogsheads of tobacco making seventy-five hundredweight, which I saw him sell for eleven écus a barrel, & it had never been so cheap. A hogshead is 500 pounds.

ON WILD AND DOMESTIC ANIMALS

HE domestic animals are exactly like those of Europe. They raise great numbers of horses, oxen, cows, sheep, pigs, turkeys, geese, ducks, chickens, & it costs nothing to keep or feed them. They do not know what it is to mow hay; their animals all graze in the woods or on the untilled portions of their plantations, where they seek shelter nightly rather by instinct than from any care given them. Grass grows so fast in this country that the same year the land is left untilled, the meadow grass is as high as in Europe after four or five years, & it makes their estates even more attractive. Pigeons are raised only by people of quality, the common people scorning such small animals. About the end of January snow lay on the ground for three days & the north wind kept blowing, so that it was very cold, but their cattle were given no care. I would see them in the morning covered with snow, shivering with cold, & eating wood because the grass was entirely hidden. Corn was fed to the pigs, & with all that, I never saw one die from it. The fowls roost in the trees around the house. To make the cows return for milking, they keep the calves inclosed in an orchard; they take what milk they want & the calves suckle the rest. They make excellent butter, but their cheese is no good. If the cattle are badly cared for, neither are they worked, save the horses, which they ride to church though it be but five hundred steps distant. As to cattle raised for food, however rapidly they may multiply, their number is kept down, for there is not a house so poor that they do not salt an ox, a cow & five or six large hogs. The women ride their horses at such a gallop when travelling that I marvelled they could keep so well seated.

As for wild animals, there are such great numbers of red & fallow deer that you cannot enter a house without being served venison. It is very good in pies, boiled or baked. There are bears, also, but not many; there are beavers & raccoons, the meat of which is excellent. Hares are somewhat scarce; the rabbits are not unlike those of Europe. There are flying squirrels that are like the others, but with wings of skin like bats. There is a prodigious abundance of birds, & to begin with the largest, there are plenty of wild turkeys, weighing from thirty-five to forty pounds. Wild geese are seen upon the seashore or along the rivers in flocks of four thousand at a time. They are larger than the domestic & almost black. There are flocks of ducks, ten thousand strong. There are also many doves, turtle-doves, thrushes, partridges in such numbers that they come into the court-yards; they are smaller than those of Europe, but taste the same. The plumage of all these birds differs from those of Europe, & I have seen none like our ravens & blackbirds. All these birds, from the big ducks down to the smallest, are immune from the pursuit of hunters, & they would not even shoot the ducks if they were not sure to kill three or four with one shot. They have many small birds that we do not have in Europe. Some are as large as larks & red all over, others as small as sparrows & quite blue, & others no larger than a big fly with feathers the colors of the rainbow.[1] This little animal feeds on dew & the juice of fragrant flowers & smells so sweet that Englishmen who came here, I was told, had them dressed & dried in an oven to sell later in England for as much as eight pounds sterling apiece, because of their sweet odor. They also have bees, so they make wax candles & eat the honey.

Fish too is wonderfully plentiful; there are so many shell oysters that almost every Saturday my host craved them.[2] He had only to send one of his servants in one of the small boats & two hours after ebb-tide he brought it back full. These boats, made of a single tree hollowed in the middle, can hold as many as fourteen people & twenty-five hundredweight of merchandise.

---

[1]Probably the cardinal, the indigo bird, and the humming bird.

[2]For the enumeration of the fish of Virginia see Beverley, Book II, Ch. V., and for the "wild fowl," Ch. VI. Curiously enough, Beverley does not mention the oysters.

THE TREES OF VIRGINIA

THE soil of this country is entirely covered with trees, excepting the tilled lands, where they have been cut. There are also great areas, twenty or twenty-five leagues from the sea; these are the fine meadows where, six or seven years ago, the savages had their plantations. It is most pleasant to walk through these woods. The trees bear no branches close to the ground, but are tall & straight & their limbs start high along the trunk; there being neither bushes nor thickets nor any kind of stones in the soil one can drive with ease anywhere.

Along the seashore are quantities of fir trees, extremely high & straight, which are used to make ship-masts; their needles are very long. There are live oaks & other oaks such as those we have, & I have seen mistletoe on some of them. There are also many chest-nut trees & three varieties of walnut trees, their leaves & wood different from those of Europe. Their nuts cannot be shelled, but they would be good to make oil.[1] There are also cedars, but not as beautiful as those

---

[1] Probably the hickory-nut, of which Beverley says, "Some of these nuts are inclosed in so hard a shell, that a light hammer will hardly crack them."

of Carolina. Its wood does not decay & is fine for making furniture; there are also quantities of poplars, the wood is very good for making planks. Trees bearing long clusters of pepper are also to be found there. And mulberry trees in abundance grow chiefly in the southern provinces. There are quantities of a kind of tree that bears fruit as large as apples. Its flavor is excellent & it is pleasant to see.[1] There are also fig trees that bear black, red, & white fruit, & grape-vines are found in greater abundance along the seashore & rivers than in the woods. They encircle around five or six trees & bear quantities of grapes, but the grapes are small as if the vines were never pruned or cultivated.[2] I found some wild grapes close to my room. I had my servant pick them & made ten or twelve jugs of juice which I left to ferment, & it was very good. But I saw most of them in the county of Rappahannock & Estaford [Stafford], chiefly on the Wormeley plantations, along the southern shore of the river. They are not cultivated; & the savages had left peach & plum trees, but cut the rest, so that these vines encircled the trees near them, & when they found no more, they

---

[1] Probably the "persimmon" described by Beverley, Book II, Ch. IV.

[2] Beverley distinguished no less than "six very different kinds" of grapes which grow with an extraordinary exuberance. He also recalls how, in 1622, "French vignerons were sent thither to make an experiment of their vines," and how the French refugees attempted, at the end of the seventeenth century, to develop a systematic cultivation of the grapevines.

stretched along the ground, between the stones & buried themselves in, in such a way that they look as if they had been planted, & on the other shore it was the same thing, but the servants told me that when he established his plantations they had uprooted more than twenty cart-loads to plant tobacco. Good wine could certainly be obtained if on arriving the branches were pruned & cultivated; at least there would be enough for one's own use, & yet low grape-vines could be planted, the wine would be better, & it would bring a very good income. There are many pears, apples, cherries, apricots & peaches on everyone's plantation. I have seen no olive trees, but if brought over they would thrive, for they can grow wherever live oaks grow.

I shall not dwell on Maryland, because its soil & trees are the same, the only difference being in temperature, as it is north of Virginia.

SEVENTH VOYAGE

A TRIP DOWN INTO THE COUNTY OF GLOUCESTER

THE place where we landed in the county of Gloster [Gloucester] is one of the most beautiful in all Virginia, but it is not the most healthful or inhabited by the most honest people. There are indeed no persons of quality. The Frenchman called for me at the ship with his small boat, for seven or eight days, but I became tired of this & decided to take a room until the ship should be repaired. I was asked four écus a month, so I resolved to stay on the vessel, but after a few days, when a new mast had been set upon the prow, she leaked so freely that two men were kept at the pumps night & day, then she had to be beached upon the sand at low tide, in order to careen her; & the leak being at the bottom, it was necessary to unload the cargo to beach her closer to the shore. Then I had to rent a room at whatever price I could, to take care of my baggage. I was obliged to pay two & a half écus a month. This Frenchman now began to take me visiting to many houses; it was cidermaking time. Everywhere we were required to drink so freely that even if there were twenty, all would drink to a stranger & he must pledge them all. They drank also some bottles of a rhum much stronger than brandy. When they were not intoxicated they usually let me drink in my own way, & generally I just kissed the glass; but when they were drunk they would have me drink at their will. This so much annoyed me that as soon as I had a room, I went no more. The cider made me ill; I think this was because it was too new. Their water also made me ill, so that time hung heavily on my hands. They worked steadily to repair the ship, but the leak in the bottom delayed them long; indeed the damage was so great that all wondered she had been able to bring us so far.

Four or five days after finding my lodgings, Monsieur Isné, who had asked to be landed in the county of Gemrive with the other merchants, heard of our shipwreck & arrived at Point Comfort in the county of Gloster [Gloucester], as this part [of Virginia] is called. He was going to see the Governor & had the kindness to go five or six leagues out of his way in order to see me & advise me against going to Carolina. He told me things I do not write down, because I do not believe them possible. However, he had not invented them, for some of the people I had seen previously had told me as much; but he could not prevail upon me & after spending the night with me he left, thinking we should never meet again, & we embraced very affectionately.

All these unfavorable reports about Carolina discouraged two more merchants & the carpenter. They had persisted so far because their passage was paid for, but they heard so many stories that they withdrew all their belongings & made what establishments they could in the county of Gloster. The captain also sold for tobacco all those women, as well as the rascals that were left, for some of them had died at sea.[1] Thus I was left to make the trip alone, with that cruel man, but my longing to be with French people overcame all these difficulties. My lodging was near the shore, & I noticed that the inhabitants of the neighborhood looked so sickly that I judged the country to be unhealthy. Those honest people forced me to drink their cider willy-nilly, but had I wished to buy some, they would have charged me six sols a jug, while charging each other but two; therefore, although it made me ill, I drank only water. I could have stood it if it had been good, for I had nothing else to drink during the last two & a half months.

Finally after five weeks spent repairing the ship, the

----

[1] These more or less voluntary passengers were the object of a regular trade, and in spite of all the efforts made to regularize their coming, abuses were frequent. This is P. A. Bruce's conclusion on the subject: "The big body of servants procured by the merchants by legitimate methods, or methods wholly illegitimate, were annually exported as a mere species of merchandise which, like the remainder of the cargo, was to be exchanged for the principal commodity of Virginia, subject to all risks attending the fluctuations in the price of tobacco." *Economic History,* I, p. 621.

pilot came to my lodging to inform me that we would sail two days hence. The next day I was ready to have my clothes taken on board, though I suffered from weakness & a languor that nearly exhausted me; but that same evening I ran a fever, so I told him that I was not fit to undertake the sea-voyage, as he well saw. He went at the time he had set & God willed that three days later the fever left me, & although I was, as before, very weak, nevertheless I could leave my bed & walk.

Monsieur Ysné, who could not have foreseen what was to befall him at the Governor's house, had gone out of his way to try to have me stop with him, & he told me he was boarding at the home of Monsieur Servent,[1] of la Rochelle, a very honest Frenchman settled for thirty-five years in the country of Gemrive.

When I reflected upon my destiny & recalled that we had been shipwrecked within sight of the coast of Carolina, the warnings given me from all sides, Monsieur Ysné's attempts to have me abandon my plan, & lastly the fever God had sent upon me to keep me abed as long as necessary to make me lose all hope of getting on board that ship, thenceforth I believed Heaven itself

---

[1]Bertrand Servent or Servant, was naturalized in 1698, and at that time indicated as being 66 years old (*William and Mary Quarterly*, XXVII, p. 136); consequently, in 1686, he was 54. His will was probated in 1707. He lived at Downes Fields, near Old Point Comfort, was a highly respected member of the colony, and held several offices even before his naturalization.

had a hand in these obstacles, & I felt convinced of it when, about two months later, we heard that the ship had been lost in the same gulf while sailing towards Carolina. I no longer persisted in my determination to go to this country, & recognized that God called me elsewhere. Meanwhile the time hung heavily on my hands; I could not talk with anyone because I did not know the language, & even if I had understood them, I would hardly have been better off for in this section there were only peasants, who were the worst scoundrels in Virginia. I resolved therefore to go to Monsieur Ysné's & if I should see fit to stop with him, to send for my belongings later. By land it was thirty leagues away, by sea it was shorter, but I did not wish to bear the expense of going alone, as for this I was asked three pistoles. I was too weak to undertake such a journey on foot, so I strolled by the seashore taking the most attractive walks in the world. Sometimes I wandered afar. My servant was only twenty; he was beginning to speak English, & I asked everywhere whether someone was going to the county of Gemrive by sea; while entertaining myself in this fashion, I discovered that nature had delighted in giving to this land many useful charms, one of them being that at various points the sea extends into the land small inlets of a hundred & fifty to two hundred feet wide. Some extend in half a league, others less. The Indians have settled along these inlets, which they call Criks. On some there is only one plantation on each shore of the creek; but larger ones, which go farther inland, have as many as five or six. What they call the North river is an inlet of the Bées sea, which extends five leagues into the county of Gloucester & is three leagues wide. It is used in the same way by the inhabitants, as are also the four rivers, all along their course. Naturally the creeks made by the rivers are farther apart, but they are much longer & I have seen some extending two leagues into the land. As their houses are at most a hundred or fifty feet distant from these creeks, at ebb-tide they not only visit in their small boats, but carry their traffic through this channel, so that their horses & oxen do not work, except when they take a fancy to work them, or when the wind is high & they go by land & ride. These are so many little havens for the launches that come to load the casks of tobacco.

After inquiring for several days I finally found a man in my neighborhood who was going to the county of Gemrive, two leagues from Monsieur Servent's, which is the name of the Frenchman with whom Monsieur Ysné had taken lodgings. He proved to be so honest that he would take no money for carrying me there, & we arrived at daybreak in this province. A Norman who had served his indenture was forthwith sent for, to take me to this Monsieur Servent's house. He was a very handsome man who had also held some office in the country. I at once enquired whether Monsieur Ysné did not live with him; he replied that as I knew him only as Monsieur Ysné, he would tell me in a few words what had happened.

He thereupon related that after living for nearly five weeks in his house, one day when they were talking together along the shore they met one of the Governor's servants, who had brought orders to the warships which lay near by the Cap de Bées. He was recognized by this servant, whom he tried his best to persuade he was a merchant & not the man he was taken for. This boy pretended to have been mistaken, but as soon as he had returned, he told his master that he had seen Milord Parker in the county of Gemrive, where he passed as a merchant & went by the name of Monsieur Ysné. To assure himself of the truth, the Governor sent for him the very next day, as though he really believed him to be a merchant, saying that it was reported that he had unloaded merchandise without due notice, that he wished to be informed of his reason for violating the county regulations, & that he must come in person immediately, to explain. Monsieur Ysné accordingly went, was recognized, & the Governor made him promise to come stay with him, giving him time only to fetch his belongings. He lent him horses & servants to go with him & unbeknownst to him wrote me a note telling me to pay Monsieur Ysné the deference due Milord Parker, as he was indeed no other person. He came to get his clothes & I helped him to dispose, at a sacrifice,

of such merchandise as he had left; he departed &
went to live in the county of Mildesse [Middlesex], almost forty leagues away. When Monsieur Servent had
concluded his tale, I replied that surely I had found in
Monsieur Isné qualities & perfections which led me
to believe he was something more than he pretended to
be; & that if during our voyage my mind had not
been so disturbed by too great a sorrow, when he told
me, on the ocean, of his intimacy while at Grenoble
with one of the most beautiful young women of our
province, who was also of high rank, I should doubtless
have suspected something; but at the time he spoke of
it, I was so concerned otherwise that I had not reflected
upon it until I had landed & was left alone.

I stopped but a day & a half at Monsieur Servent's, because his wife was ill. I no longer thought of
staying with him after I heard Mr. Isné's story, so I
walked back to find my guide. When I came upon him
he was in the company of seven or eight of his friends.
He was from this province, & had come to visit his
relations. They all told me that I must carouse with
them for seven or eight days, & after that, he would
take me back in his boat. I did not feel so inclined.
The Norman was in their midst; I started on the road I
had to follow to return by land, & after being given
the name of a house where I could spend the night &
all directions for the journey, I left them.

One travels very comfortably & cheaply in this

country.[1] There are no inns but everywhere I went I was welcome. They cordially gave me to eat & to drink of whatever they had, & if I slept in a house where they owned horses, on the morrow some were lent to me to use for the first half of the next day's journey. My leanness now stood me in good stead, for in France I should certainly have found it hard to walk two leagues, whereas here I was so gaunt that I could do six or seven easily. It is true, however, one can always keep to the flat country, through woods & meadows, unhindered by either stones or mud. In this way, I crossed three of these southern provinces, & noticed quantities of mulberry-trees, & I observed that the soil was less productive than in the county of Gloucester, because it is more sandy. I crossed the York river opposite a brick fort, where there are 20 or 25 fine guns.[2] The Gover-

---

[1]This Virginia hospitality, so pleasantly maintained by the old families, is, as one may see here, a tradition dating from the beginnings of the colony. "The inhabitants are very courteous to travellers, who need no other recommendation, but the being human creatures. A stranger has no more to do, but to inquire upon the road, where any gentleman, or good housekeeper lives, and there he may depend upon being received with hospitality. This good nature is so general among their people, that the Gentry when they go abroad, order their principal servant to entertain all visitors, with everything the plantation affords. And the poor planters, who have but one bed, will very often sit up, or lie upon a form of couch all night, to make room for a weary traveller, to repose himself after his journey." Beverley, Book IV, Ch. XXI.

[2]This was probably Fort James established in 1667, and rebuilt in bricks in 1672. In 1668 it was described as "a silly sort of a fort, that is a brick wall in the shape of a half-moon." According to the

nor's house is very near, but he no longer lives there, because last summer, in two months, he lost his lady, two pages, & five or six men servants or maids, in consequence he had removed his residence to the house of Monsieur Wormeley, in the county of Mildessex [Middlesex], 16 or 18 leagues from that place, where he keeps in good health.[1] Beyond the river I found myself in the province of Gloucester, eight leagues from Point Comfort, where I arrived as best I could, almost exhausted after travelling thirty leagues on foot.

A few days after returning to my room [I was visited by] a good French boy from Abeville in Picardy, who, having finished his service, had become a Lieutenant & thereby saved some money. He was about to be married two leagues away from my lodgings & as he had been to see me before, he came to invite me to his wedding. He had become a Protestant & was marrying a good girl of a very decent family. On his wedding-day, then, he sent two of his father-in-law's negroes for me in a boat, & I went by water. The In-

---

editor of *A Frenchman in Virginia,* it seems certain that the guns which Durand mentions had not been mounted at that date.

[1] The Governor of Virginia was then Francis Howard of Effingham, who resided in the colony from 1683 to 1688, and whose elder brother was in command of the fleet which defeated the Armada. On several occasions he complained of the diseases brought on by the heat of summer, and he was accustomed to seek "some more healthy climate" during the hot season. See P. A. Bruce, *Economic History,* I, p. 139.

dians[1] make a great festival of a wedding. There were at least a hundred guests, many of social standing, & handsome, well-dressed ladies. Although it was November, we ate under the trees. The day was perfect. We were twenty-four at the first table. They served us so copiously with meats of all kinds that I am sure there would have been enough for a regiment of five hundred soldiers, even entirely made up of men from Languedoc, Provence, or Dauphiné. The Indians eat almost no bread, seldom drink during meals; but they did nothing afterwards, for the rest of the day & all night, but drink, smoke, sing & dance. They had no wine; they drank beer, cider, & punch, a mixture prepared in a large bowl. They put in three jugs of beer, three jugs of brandy, three pounds of sugar, some nutmegs & cinnamon, mix these well together & when the sugar has melted they drink it, & while making away with the first, they prepare another bowl of it. As for me, I drank beer only, cider makes me ill & I do not care for sugar. It is the custom to take only one meal upon such occasions, at two o'clock in the afternoon.[2] They do not provide beds for the men;

---

[1] In several places Durand uses the term "Indiens" when he evidently meant those who, in France, were called the "Anglo-Américains" or colonists born in America.

[2] According to Mr. Philip A. Bruce (*Social Life in Virginia*, p. 255) no seventeenth century description is available of the festivities following the celebration of a wedding; on the other hand, one may find, in the same work, precise indications on the banquet following

[138]

those available are for the women & girls, so that about midnight, after much carousing, when some were already lying on the floor, I fell asleep in a chair close by the fire. The master of the house saw me & took me to the room of the women & girls, where four or five cots had been arranged, also feather beds. Collecting all the blankets, he laid me a bed on the floor, saying he would not put it in the hall for fear the drunken fellows would fall over me & keep me from sleeping. They caroused all night long & when it was day I got up. I did not see one who could stand straight. A little later the bridegroom arose, gave me a good breakfast, & had me taken back to my lodgings by his slave.

---

a funeral. In 1667, after a funeral, the mourners consumed 25 gallons of beer, 22 of cider, 5 of brandy, and 12 pounds of sugar. Such are the ingredients which were used to make the "ponch" according to the recipe given by Durand.

THE EIGHTH VOYAGE

A TRIP TO THE COUNTIES OF PIANKETANK, MIDDLESEX, NORTHUMBERLAND, RAPPAHANNOCK, STAFFORD & MARYLAND[1]

I WAS very anxious to see Monsieur Isné, whom henceforth I shall call Monsieur Parker. I was curious to know how he would behave towards me, after being recognized for what he was. I was but eleven leagues from the county of Mildessex, but as I had to go on foot, I still felt too weak & exhausted to undertake the journey. So I rested until the 17th of December.

Up to that time I had not decided upon an establishment, for while I was delighted with the country, I could not see any possibility of settling in it. I had not left my native land to spend the rest of my life deprived of the exercise of my religion, as I should have had to do there, or at least it would have been in what was to me an utterly barbaric language. As for Carolina, I had en-

---

[1]Durand wrote Peyquetan, Mildessex, Notomberland, Rappahannak, Estafort and Marilan.

tirely abandoned my plan to go there, & realized that it would have been tempting God to persevere in this project after the great obstacles he had put in my path. I knew that in the northern colonies there were many Frenchmen & even some ministers, but the cold climate discouraged me almost as much as the heat of Carolina. I was determined to let January go by before leaving Virginia, both on account of cold weather & the danger in passing the Cape in that season; a ship loaded with negroes had been wrecked there five or six days before. Meanwhile I humbled myself before God & besought him to advise me in my doubts, & help me in all my uncertainties.

Still undecided, I set out, & went to spend the night with a physician six leagues from my lodgings. He put me up very comfortably & the next day lent me horses to take me to Monsieur Wormeley's, which was not more than five leagues away.[1] Monsieur

---

[1] Ralph Wormeley of Rosegill (1650–1700), whose mother had married Sir Henry Chicherley, deputy-governor of Culpeper, was, consequently, not the son, but the step-son of "the late governor." Sir Ralph had been brought up in England, and had studied at Oxford. He was president of the "Council" in 1688, and became "secretary of the colony" in 1693. During his life he was considered the most important person in Virginia, after the governor. The residence he built, which he called "Rosegill," still remains as one of the purest examples of seventeenth century colonial architecture. In its original condition, the main house included a parlor, two rooms and a nursery on the first floor, with three bed-rooms and a store room on the second floor. The kitchen, dairy, and servants' quarters were, as usual, in separate buildings. P. A. Bruce,

Wormeley is the son of the late Governor, he is a Baronet, & although he still possesses estates in England, he has settled in this country. He owns twenty-six negro slaves & twenty Christian. He holds the highest offices, & owns at least twenty houses in a lovely plain along the Rappahannock river. He has rented his most comfortable house to the Governor.[1] When I reached his place I thought I was entering a rather large village, but later on was told that all of it belonged to him. I met Milord Parker in the courtyard. He received me with great affection & introduced me to the Governor, to whom I paid my respects. I then drew him aside, in a corner of the room, & told him I wished in some manner to apologize for the lack of courtesy & too great familiarity with which I had treated him. This, however, could be excused, for he had brought it upon himself through the special care he had taken to keep me in this error. He replied most pleasantly that even if I had recognized him for what he really was, he would have been sorry to exact more courtesy than I had shown, & he begged me, if I wished to please him, to behave in the future with the same familiarity as before. In truth he had taken such pains to hide his rank that he had left his retinue with his

Economic Life in Virginia, Vol. II, "Records of Middlesex County," p. 156.

[1]The "Virginian" has found a document signed from Rosegill by the Governor, in September, 1686, which confirms the assertion of Durand.

Plate V.   ROSEGILL: *The Hall*

mother, & had written one of his friends in London that he was sailing on our vessel, taking along three or four tons of merchandise of all sorts, & even earthenware; & to send him a man-servant taken from jail & condemned to banishment. This servant believed him to be a real merchant all the while he served him.

The table was immediately set, & after dinner his Excellency asked me what I thought of the country. I told him I considered it very fine & very beautiful, & if the preaching were in French, I would spend there the rest of my life, but that the difference of language would force me either to return to Europe, or to settle in the northern colonies. He replied that he had orders to give each foreigner wishing to settle in his "government" fifty acres of land, but inasmuch as I had left my country for the Religion, as well as because I was recommended by Monsieur Parker, he would give me five hundred, but I would have to settle further back & be among the savages, who, he added, are not greatly to be feared, but there is some inconvenience owing to the fact that only small boats can sail up the rivers in the back country so one could not trade by water. For this reason, as there are vast tracts of land for sale very cheap, very good & among Christians, he advised me to buy there, rather than further away. He believed this climate would suit Frenchmen better than Carolina which is too hot, or Pennsylvania & New England, because of the cold. He had lately received news that there were great numbers [of French people] in England & more kept coming, so that if I wished to return & bring them with ministers, he would serve us to the best of his ability, & as for the pastors, provided that from time to time they preached in English & baptized & married the other Christians who might be among the French settlers, he would give benefices to two or three, & they would be required to read the book of common prayers when preaching, except when they preached to French people only, they could then do as they were accustomed in France. There was nothing extraordinary in his offer of these lands, except the amount, for in all places under English rule they give each stranger fifty acres out of the land not yet taken up by the inhabitants. I gave him my best thanks for his kind offers & answered that it was a long journey for a man of my years, already weakened by the long voyage to America, but nevertheless I would think it over & decide in a few days whether my health would permit me to undertake it.

Hereupon some strangers came in, & Monsieur Parker took this opportunity to go walking with me along the river.[1] It was a beautiful day. He felt my desire to know why he had concealed his rank. He did not wait for me to ask, but as soon as we were alone, related that two or three years back, while at Grenoble, he had fallen in love with Mademoiselle Marie de la

---

[1]On this episode see *Introduction,* p. 35.

Garene. When this young lady & her mother had expressed the wish to see Lyons & Paris, & he had been obliging enough to take them there. They had remained a couple of months in Lyons, & eighteen or twenty in Paris, spending lavishly, keeping a fine carriage & large establishment, & to provide for all this, he had drawn his income two years ahead, which length of time he had resolved to pass in America to recoup his fortune, unknown & as a merchant, so he could spend less. "Now that I know who you are," I answered, "I am convinced of the truth of all you related to me during our voyage, concerning this young lady, but you must excuse me if when I believed you to be a merchant, & knowing her to be beautiful, proud & of high rank, I had not given it much credence." "Well," he went on, "in order to remove all of your doubts & also because I still enjoy speaking of her. . ." He then ordered one of his servants to bring him a casket out of which he took four letters that he requested me to read. They were written in a tender & passionate style; & when I was reading the last one, in which she intimated that were she so unfortunate as to discover that she had lost his love, far from giving her affections to another, she would retire into a convent for the rest of her days, he stopped me at this point & said, "Yet she has not kept her word, for a few days before leaving for America, I learned on good authority that the Archbishop of Paris had fallen in love with her,

& has secretly kept her in a more magnificent style than I did, for which I am well pleased," he added, "for I still love her a little, & I should have dreaded for her to fall into want, after spending the forty pistoles I left with her at my departure. But now I fear nothing on this score, because this good prelate is so charitable that he will let her want for nothing."—"As you take pleasure in speaking of her," I replied, "I shall now relate to you in a few words the fatal results wrought by her beauty upon a man two leagues from my house. He was a handsome gentleman, the sole male heir, & he had but one sister, married a few years before; his father possessed an income of ten thousand pounds; being deeply in love, he prevailed upon all those he thought capable of influencing his father & mother to induce them to permit him to marry her. But these good people, while they could raise no objection against her rank or her family, yet because of their love of wealth, although she was far from penniless, & their expectations for their son, were deterred from giving their consent. This reduced the young man to such despair that he rushed into the Carthusian monastery at Lyons, where the good fathers made so much of him that his father & mother have been powerless ever to get him back. Thus, to our great regret, her beauty has caused one of my neighbors to withdraw from the world; but I judge that his sister, who already had five or six children & whose husband had squandered part of their for-

tune, being none too thrifty, will be easily consoled."
Monsieur Parker said she had told him all this, but he
had not credited it, thinking she was boasting a little,
but now he felt more inclined to believe it.

I stayed a day & a half with these gentlemen, after
which I wished to leave. Monsieur Parker told me that
for the present he would not urge me to remain, because
the next day he was going on a visit ten leagues away,
but that I should hold myself in readiness the following
week, as he would send me his horses, for as soon as he
was recognized he had bought three good ones. I did
not decline this offer, as I was very tired of being so
much alone. Having borrowed some horses, I departed
& sent them back from the Painquetain [Piakatank]
river, half way to Point Comfort, which has to be
crossed by boat. He did not fail to send the horses at
the appointed time, & the next day I went to him. I
stayed five or six days; we took our meals once a day
with the Governor, at two o'clock in the afternoon.
This is the only meal he takes regularly at home, the
others at Monsieur Wormeley's. He had us served
white wine from Spain and claret from Portugal, &
Monsieur Wormeley wine from Portugal, cider &
beer. As it was now nearly five months that I had drunk
nothing but water, I found these wines so strong that I
asked leave to dilute them with an equal quantity of
water. The Governor & Monsieur Wormeley laughed
at me, but Monsieur Parker, who had travelled ex-

tensively in France, having tasted it decided to always drink it the same way, & in fact, I still found it as strong as the best wine we have in France undiluted.

The Parliament sat during this time. They usually assemble in extraordinary session when there is important business. A ship from Guiana, loaded with negroes, had violated the law. She was taken by men-of-war, tried & confiscated. I saw there fine-looking men, sitting in judgment booted & with belted sword. What caused me to say that people of quality handle money, is that after supper they started gambling & it was close on towards midnight when Monsieur Parker, who had insisted I should always sleep with him, noticed I was waiting. He begged me to retire & go to bed. "For," said he, "it is quite possible that we shall be here all night," & in truth I found them still playing the next morning, & saw that he had won a hundred écus from them.

When the meeting of Parliament was over, I saw that Monsieur Wormeley made ready for a journey to the County of Rappahannock, where he had plantations twenty-two leagues away, so I wished to depart. Having acquainted Monsieur Parker with my decision while we were still abed, he replied that he had not had me fetched for so short a time; that we should spend the Christmas holidays together & he expected me to go with him. I very readily accepted & the next day Monsieur Wormeley gave me a good horse & another for my servant, & we started only two hours before dark. The Governor, who is a very sociable man, would not let us leave until we had dined with him. One travels so fast in this country that in two hours we had covered about six leagues. The horses are so used to this quick pace that once upon their backs one has nothing to do but to hold on. I do not believe there are better horses in the world, & none so badly used, for it was the 29th of December according to French style, but as this is the end of my almanach henceforth I shall count according to the old calendar, as they do in the Indies. Their saddles only were taken off, after they had been fed a little Indian corn, & thus all lathered with sweat they were driven into the woods, where they ate whatever they could find, though it was freezing hard. Our lodgings were not especially good that night, which caused us to take our departure early the next morning. We rode six leagues further, at the same quick pace; we stopped at the house of an honest man who gave us good food & clean lodgings. We slept there. There was no reason to hurry, for Monsieur Wormeley had sent his launch ahead, loaded with supplies, & as the wind was not blowing she could only move forward with the flood tide. The next day we came to some hills. We were in the county of Northumberland, & as we approached the river, which had to be crossed in boats, Monsieur Wormeley had someone tell me that there lived in the vicinity the widow of a bourgeois, only thirty years of

[149]

age, good-looking, childless, & that he knew she wanted nothing better than to marry a man of quality. He had great influence with her. She had a good house, a plantation of a thousand acres of land, with cattle of all kinds; it was hardly a league from where we stood & if I agreed to it, we could turn off there, & he would propose me to her as a husband. Marriage was the last thing I thought of. This would indeed have been a fortune for me, but the difference in language which was compelling me to leave this country also forced me to [decline the honor] & thank him for the care he was taking of my establishment; thus we continued on our way, & although I refused these proposals, I could not but admire the ways of Providence, & the trustworthiness of the promises made us by our Lord in his Evangel, when He said that unto those who leave all to follow Him, He will grant much more, & lastly life eternal, for in this distant clime, where I was fearful when cast ashore, that I should find none to give me shelter, He had brought forth the most illustrious in all America to be my friends, & a match worth a thousand acres of land, with many other good things.

And so we crossed the river to enter the province of Rappahannock. We stopped with the County Judge. His houses stood along the river. There we met the launch, driven up by the tide during the night, & the next day we went to Portobago, as they call Monsieur Wormeley's fine plantations. The Judge, with one of his friends who happened to be there, & the honest man with whom we had formerly lodged, all came along with us.

The launch had brought all kinds of supplies except meat, which she was to carry back. The gentlemen immediately had bowls of punch prepared, & they began to carouse, while I went walking, delighted with the sight of those lovely hills, the fountains & brooks flowing out of them, as well as with the quantity of wild grapevines all about. On this side I counted eight or nine houses that Monsieur Wormeley has built on his estates or plantations. His cattle seemed to me fatter & bigger than any I had seen in the county of Gloucester or elsewhere in the country. I noticed also that about two-thirds of the lands were wooded, the other meadows which were, as I have already mentioned, the plantations that belonged to the savages five or six years ago; three of these savages came to visit him as soon as we had arrived.[1] They brought him two wild turkeys & a domestic one. The wild turkeys surely weighed 40 pounds each. We could see their village on the opposite bank of the river, so the next day, having

---

[1]On the whole, Beverley confirms the sketchy indications of Durand. Even at this early date, very few Indians remained near the English settlements; their number was estimated at five hundred. The natives formed small villages constituted by two or three families. In 1705 the native population of Port Tobago, where Wormeley had established a plantation, was "about five bowmen, but wasting." Beverley, III, Ch. XIII.

expressed a wish to see them at home, Monsieur Wormeley had three horses taken across the river, & ordered an early dinner. Monsieur Parker, Monsieur Wormeley & I got into the boat that had been sent back for us, & then mounted the horses. We rode over all the lands on this side of the river, which are greater in extent than those on the north side, where we had our quarters. I counted six houses & saw a great abundance of wild grapevines trailing along the ground & so many peach trees that when they are ripe, so they told me, the hogs will not budge from them as long as they last, not even to drink, for they are always drunk, & that they fatten better than on acorns & chestnuts. After having gone all over this section, we went to the village of the savages.

These savages have rather pretty houses, the walls as well as the roofs ornamented with trees, & so securely fastened together with deer thongs that neither rain nor wind causes them inconvenience. These people are darker than the Egyptians we see in Europe. They brand their faces with scars in the shape of snail-shells, into which they put powder & so are marked for life. The women, in the house wear only a deer skin to cover the less mentionable parts. In winter they wear the fur against their skin, & in summer the skin against their skin. They build their fire in the center of the house, their beds are made all around. They interweave a kind of strong, coarse grass that grows along the river to

Plate VI. AN INDIAN VILLAGE—from BEVERLEY: *History of Virginia*

Plate VII.   INDIAN WOMEN—from BEVERLEY: *History of Virginia*

make a sort of mat, held up by four little forks. They use these as seats. The men in the village wear only a shabby shirt of blue or white linen, & from the time they put it on they do not remove it until it falls in rags, for they never wash anything. Except for this fur, the women have the rest of their bodies nude. The little children are always entirely naked, however cold it may be. The men do nothing but hunt, & fish, while the women plant Indian corn. The crop belongs to the community, each taking whatever he needs. The women also make pots, earthen vases & smoking pipes. The Christians buying these pots or vases fill them with Indian corn, which is the price of them. They all smoke, as do the men, but as they grow no tobacco, they give game or fish in exchange for it. They marry only to avoid confusing the parentage of their children; as soon as a young man has taken a wife, he builds a small house & leaving his father & mother, goes to live in it. They have some knowledge, but a very imperfect one, of the true God; they believe Him to be the author of what they see & of the productions of the earth necessary to their life, but that He is not concerned in their conduct & that He does not stoop so low; that Demons inferior to Him were created for this purpose, & these they fear, being from time to time abused by them. They have no other marriage ceremony than to have the village assemble & the young man, after choosing her he wishes for his wife, gives her a hind or hart foot, while she offers him an ear of Indian corn, signifying that the husband will provide the house with meat & the wife with corn. The ministers in this country take no pains to convert them to Christianity or to instruct them, although most of them know how to speak English. When we left they gave Monsieur Wormeley a dozen deer skins as a present, & Monsieur Parker & myself a handful of pipes each.

As it was already night, we had the boat come in order to return; it took some time to cross for the river is very wide, & at this point it is navigable by vessels of a hundred & twenty tons, although thirty leagues distant from the sea. Meanwhile I was extolling upon the beauty of the place we had just seen, the same lovely hills whence flow fountains & brooks, & broad meadows below, always covered with wild grapevines; I was saying that fine vines could grow upon these slopes & that doubtless the wine would be excellent. Thereupon Monsieur Wormeley replied that if I could find some means to bring Frenchmen there, he would sell the whole of those ten thousand acres of ground he owned on both sides of the river for one écu an acre, that he would give for the same price & in addition to the houses, fourteen of them I think, the fenced lands and the tilled lands upon his domains. But the cattle would have to be paid for separately, & he offered credit for two or three years to those who had not the money to pay with when taking possession; he would lend them for their support during the first year all the corn that he should harvest there; & he would serve them to the best of his ability, for, he continued, this is far from my house & I own ten thousand acres more in the county of Middlesex.

Until then I had hesitated & questioned whether to go back to England, or to the north of America, but when I saw the beauty & fertility of the Rappahannock province, & especially of Monsieur Wormeley's lands, this added to the satisfaction I had enjoyed those last days, which had certainly helped me to recover part of my strength, all led me to decide positively to return to Europe. I realized that this country was unknown & as it had no proprietors, no one had taken the trouble to print accounts of it, such as those of Carolina & Pennsylvania. I even deemed it possible that the great obstacles I encountered when planning to go & settle in Carolina might have been foreordained so that I should inform the many poor refugees of this pleasant & healthful retreat. Charity added to other considerations urged me so that I no longer had any thought but to look for an opportunity to sail as early as possible.

Having acquainted Monsieur Parker with my intention, he encouraged me as much as he could. He asked Monsieur Wormeley to write out the agreements & to sign them with his own hand, stating that he wished to sell these lands, with the price he was asking for them; this he promised to do as soon as he returned to his house.

The Christmas holidays were drawing near; Monsieur Parker was a Roman Catholic, but not of the kind who are bigoted. He was a real man of honor, & as he had left our kingdom after Easter in the year 1686, he had witnessed with his own eyes the way we had been abused, & knowing our innocence, this had roused in him such great compassion for our misfortunes that he at all times denounced the ruthlessness of the French clergy. He wished to spend Christmas day in Maryland. As it was but five or six leagues away, we had no intention of letting him go alone. Consequently we decided to pass the night at Colonel Fichoux'[1] [Fitz-

---

[1] This is another instance of phonetic transcription. In a review of Mr. B. W. Green's *Word-Book of Virginia Folk-Speech* (Richmond, 1899), Professor J. L. Hall indicates that "Ficheux" is still the current pronunciation of Fitzhugh (*Virginia Historical Magazine*, 1899, Vol. VII, p. 219). The "Fichoux" of Durand, is William Fitzhugh of Bedford in Stafford, one of the most important proprietors of Virginia, who had received the rank of lieutenant-colonel. A few weeks before, Fitzhugh had been severely attacked in the Assembly and threatened with suspension of all his emoluments, his attitude being characterized as "an abuse upon Stafford County and the whole country" (*Journals of the House of Burgesses of Virginia, 1659–1693*, edited by H. R. McIlwaine, Richmond, Virginia, 1914). The session of the Assembly was held at James City, from October 20th to November 17, 1686.

The history of the plans for colonization favored by Fitzhugh are exceedingly complicated. It can be traced from his correspondence published in the *Virginia Historical Magazine*, 1894–1895, and a résumé of it is to be found in *the Landmarks of Old Prince William*, Vol. I, pp. 117–196. It appears that even before the Revocation of

Plate VIII.   WILLIAM FITZHUGH

hugh's], whose houses stand along the banks of the great Pethomak river.

We were delayed a few moments in starting because as we were about to take horse all those savages, men, women & little children, came to return our visit; those who had been able to procure jerkins from the Christians were wearing them, as also the women who wore some kind of petticoats, others wore some pieces of shabby blue cloth from which were made the blankets they had traded on some ships in exchange for deer skins. They had made a hole in the center to put their heads through & fastened it around their body with deer-thongs. The women were wearing theirs as a mantilla, like the Egyptian women in Europe, & their children were entirely naked. They had taken to adorn

the Edict of Nantes, Nicholas Hayward, son of a London merchant and "notary public on the Virginia walk of the exchange," an entirely beloved and good friend of William Fitzhugh, had bought a plantation on the Potomac near Bedford. His intention was to bring there, as colonists, some of the Huguenot refugees who were then in London. Fitzhugh became much interested in the plan, and as Hayward's plantation seemed too small in extent, he proposed to place the refugees on a tract of land he had recently acquired on the upper Accotink. This tract, which later became Ravensworth, included no less than 22,000 acres, and, through a letter dated May, 1686, was offered for the settlement of French Protestants. Hayward had refused the proposition of Colonel Fitzhugh and persisted in his original plan. The text of his *"Proposition"* will be found at the end of this volume. This project does not seem to have succeeded, although Fitzhugh attracted to his plantation a few refugees, among whom was "a French minister." However, when he died, in 1701, he was known as the "French refugee's great friend."

themselves, some kind of pure white fishbones, slipping a strand of hair through a bone, & so on all around their head. They also wore necklaces & bracelets made of small grains which are found in the country. Beads of which rosaries are made in France were also brought over for them, & the cleanest & wealthiest took away as many as they could slip upon their necks & arms, from elbow to hand, for these are their treasures.

We left soon after, & they were sorry to see us go, for I felt they had taken great pleasure in our company. Monsieur Wormeley is so well beloved & esteemed in this county that all the honest people in the neighborhood came to see him & would not leave him, so we rode twenty strong to Colonel Fichous' [Fitzhugh's], but he has such a large establishment that he did not mind. We were all of us provided with beds, one for two men. He treated us royally, there was good wine & all kinds of beverages, so there was a great deal of carousing. He had sent for three fiddlers, a jester, a tight-rope dancer, an acrobat who tumbled around, & they gave us all the entertainment one could wish for. It was very cold, yet no one ever thinks of going near the fire, for they never put less than a cartload of wood in the fireplace & the whole room is kept warm.

As soon as we left Monsieur Wormeley's estate we entered the county of Stafford which begins here, but stretches so far between the two rivers that there are no boundaries north & west. The land is as fertile as in Rappahannock county, & although there are more hills, there are none higher. I saw great quantities of wild grapevines. A gentleman who lives in the neighborhood of the Colonel, having heard of our arrival, came over. He told us that three or four of them had twenty-five thousand acres of land for sale in this same county, six or seven leagues from the place where we were, & others who lived in London & were very honest men, had been commissioned to offer lands at a reasonable price to any Frenchman wishing to come, & even to advance money to help build houses for those who had no funds, as well as corn for their sustenance during the first year.

The next day, after they had caroused until after noon, we decided to cross this river. The Colonel had a quantity of wine & one of his punch-bowls brought to the shore; he lent us his boat. We had left our horses at his place & as many of us as could get in went in the boat, the others remained. We went to spend the night at the home of a Maryland gentleman, who also treated us very well. The next day we were told the nearest Roman Catholic church was seven or eight leagues distant, & Monsieur Wormeley having business that called him back, wished to leave. As I was riding his horses, I could not stay, so to my great regret we had to part. It was Christmas eve, & Monsieur Parker wished to perform his religious exercises, but before parting he took me for a walk & said that as it was some time since I had left my country, I might be in need of something. He offered me a purse with more than a hundred English pistoles, & urged me to take what I needed without stint, adding that his Excellency when he left had earnestly commanded him to tell me that in case I resolved to return to Europe & wished to come back with Frenchmen, I could rest assured that he would do all in his power to help us, & that he wished to give me a letter of introduction to the Bishop of London, one of his relatives. As for himself, as soon as it was May he would leave to spend the two or three most dangerous months for sickness in Pennsylvania & New England; he intended to be back in Virginia in the month of October, & then he would go to spend the winter in Barbados; he desired me if I returned to try to be back about that time, so that he might have the pleasure of rendering me additional service. Moreover he declared that if he heard I was still in America when he returned from his trip to Maryland he would come to visit me. I answered that I felt overwhelmed by the favors & kindness he had shown me, but as for money, I still had enough for my voyage & could repay so much generosity only with respect & reverence during the rest of my life. After this we parted.

Monsieur Wormeley & I came back the same day in time to sleep at his plantation, where we spent Christmas day. Then we stopped with the Judge who had not left us, & thence to the house of a captain of cavalry, where we remained some time because Monsieur Wormeley, who is the Colonel of this county, wished to see his company. Then we rode back to his place by the same road we had come, & he kept me two days longer; meanwhile a shipmaster happened to visit him, who was due to leave for London at the end of January, & we agreed upon a price to carry me. His Excellency renewed the same offers of service he had tendered through Monsieur Parker, after which I left, accompanied by one of his own servants, who was to bring back the horses. This poor boy, who claimed to be the son of a minister in Montauban, & had been sold in this country three years before, caught pleurisy as soon as we arrived at my lodgings & died five days later, which caused me deep chagrin.

LAST VOYAGE

THE RETURN TO EUROPE

NOTHER consideration which contributed in no small degree to my decision to return to Europe, with which I did not acquaint Monsieur Parker because he was a Roman Catholic & consequently little conversant with the Scriptures, was that on leaving for America I had bought the accomplishment of the prophecies by Monsieur de Jurieu,[1] in which that great man sets forth with such complete evidence the present persecution through the death of two martyrs & the deliverance of the Church through their resurrection, all this with such strong & convincing proofs that after reading it two or three times I became almost as sure of this future as the past has been made certain to me by these severe trials. Therefore I wished to be a witness of the resto-

---

[1]In his *Accomplissement des Prophéties ou la Délivrance de l'Eglise*, published at Rotterdam in 1686, the famous Jurieu had predicted the reëstablishment of the Reformed Church in France for the year 1689. If we are to judge from Durand, this publication must have increased the natural reluctance of the Huguenots to settle in remote regions, and to abandon all hope of ever returning to their native country.

ration of the Religion in my country, as I had been of its affliction & its ruin.

Meanwhile I had become so provoked with my host & hostess about the death of the poor Frenchman that I could no longer endure the sight of them. They hardly waited for him to breathe his last before seizing his money & clothes, & I had to quarrel with them to save two écus to pay the surgeon who had attended him. They brazenly kept all the rest, although they had not cared for him during his illness, for my servant had all the trouble & I the expense. Therefore I began immediately to look for another lodging.

I settled two leagues away, on the road to our ship, to be near when she came along. They exacted from me the rent of my room up to the last day, at two & a half écus a month, & forced me to leave behind without credit some door locks I had put in, saying it was the law of America, that anything once fastened cannot be carried away. Thus for the four or five months I lived there, I paid enough to have them build two rooms like the one I occupied. I was so unfortunate that I went to stay with people even more uncivil & heartless than those I had left. They strove in this place to wring from me the little I still possessed by whatever means they could. I hired a woman to wash some clothes; she spent only half the day doing it, & charged me an écu. If I sent corn to their mills they shamelessly kept half of it; if I bought anything from them they charged three times more than it was worth; all of which made me so afraid that I would be unable to pay my passage & so would be forced to stay among these inhuman people that I resolved to buy nothing more from them & henceforth restricted myself to bread & water.

Meanwhile a rumor spread through the country that I was going to bring back or send Frenchmen there. Two men from Pianketank County came to offer me, one, three thousand acres of land for sale in a province twenty-five leagues away, along the York river, & the other, two thousand. They asked me twenty sols an acre, & told me they were entirely timbered lands. I cannot say whether the soil is good for I have not been there. The people in the neighborhood also came to offer me, one, seven hundred acres, another five hundred, another four hundred. To these I answered, for they brought interpreters with them, that they could be assured that because of their bad waters as well as of the manner in which they had treated me, I could never advise any Frenchmen to settle among them.

The master of the ship was so unpunctual that it was already the fifteenth of February & I had heard nothing from him. Meanwhile, either from worry or poor food, I lost the embonpoint I had gained during the four or five weeks I passed with the gentlemen, & I saw myself become exceedingly thin & weak. However, although very anxious, I waited patiently until the first of March, then unable to bear any longer the rudeness of my hosts & neighbors, I determined to leave, cost what it might, & to reach this captain eighteen leagues away. It was necessary to go by sea because of my belongings, so I found a boat for hire at twelve sols a day, but had to engage two men to manage it, the owner being sick. I found them & was obliged to promise each fifty sols a day & food.

On the eve of my departure, as Mr. Parker was destined to render me all sorts of good offices, I received from him a letter that detained me. When we took leave of each other he had, indeed, said he would come to visit me, but not daring to hope to be thus honored, I had not remembered it. He came most opportunely, however, to save me the three or four pistoles this journey would have cost. He thought I was still lodged in the same place, at the mouth of an inlet two leagues long, & being on the opposite side, to avoid the three or four leagues more he would have had to ride round, he left his horses & came by boat; upon being told that I lived two leagues farther he attempted to go on foot, but turned back, & to quiet the impatience he rightly thought possessed me, wrote that he would send me a servant a week before the ship was to pick me up, which he believed would now be very soon.

This letter compelled me to stay some time longer among these fine folk. I went no more to their churches, for after I had changed my lodgings they were three leagues distant. Sunday was the day that seemed to me the longest, & being without religious worship I yearned for the beautiful exhortations of the illustrious & excellent pastors I had left in London & made up my mind never to risk living in a place where there would not be any, even though it should reduce my means of subsistence by a half.

Monsieur Parker did not fail, eight or ten days after his return, to send me a servant as he had promised, with the kindest letter in the world, notifying me that the ship which was to carry me had arrived, & was lying opposite the Governor's house; that those gentlemen & he himself had emphatically instructed the captain to take the best of care of me during the voyage, & informing me also of the letter his Excellency had written to the Bishop of London in my behalf, & of Mr. Wormeley's proposition for the sale of his lands.

At last, on the 15th of March, at two o'clock in the afternoon, I saw four sailors & the ship's surgeon arrive. The captain was drifting slowly waiting for us, for there was little wind at the time when he sent them. In a trice they had put all my belongings in the boat & I left with great satisfaction a place which had been so strangely wearisome to me. But my joy was short-lived, for scarcely had we sailed half a league on the ocean than a high wind began blowing which put us in great danger the like of which, I may say, I had never before experienced. Our plight was such that in order to lighten the ship we had made ready to cast overboard all my belongings, for the waves were sweeping the decks, when we caught sight of a ship sailing ahead of us. I had some firearms & caused them to be discharged so repeatedly that she waited for us. We boarded her as night fell, the surgeon having jumped aboard her, held out a rope to me & I boarded her also. My servant & the sailors remained to carry out my belongings, but they had time only to bring up a small cask full of tobacco that I had taken along to make presents, & the tempest increased so much that they hardly had time to save themselves. They fastened the boat rather badly, for it was very cold, & thus I saw in great danger all that I still owned in the world. I had placed in my chests everything I had of any value, & what I deplored most was that my money was in them, & I had to give forty écus to the captain for our passage. I had given all the money I had in my pockets to pay the rent of my room, which left me without a sol; indeed I can say that all my remaining possessions including the shirt on my back did not amount even to one pistole. The shipmaster seeing me wet to the skin, sent me to lie on his bed, where I had not been two hours when the surgeon who had called for me, & my servant entered the room, both very much frightened, to tell me that we were utterly lost, that the ship's prow could no longer be seen, & that the water was reaching up to the door of the room abaft where I was. As for me, without troubling to get up to look at the danger, I knelt upon my bed & prayed to

God while waiting for the time when the boat would sink. The sailors had dropped the pro-anchor so hastily, because of the heavy storm, that they had not given it enough cable, & the wind blowing from the stern, the anchor stuck so hard into the ground that the vessel would have overturned had not God miraculously protected us, for he allowed the cable to snap & by degrees our ship righted herself.

They had lightened the ship of all that loaded her from center to prow. They came to tell us that we were out of danger, but the boat containing my belongings had been wrecked against our ship & everything lost. This news robbed me of the joy I should have felt at being saved, for I saw myself naked, destitute of everything among strangers, so that besides being wet through, I spent one of the worst nights of my life. I truly envied the martyrdom of the blessed Monsieur de Lys, a neighbor of mine half a league distant, who was beheaded while I was hiding at Marseilles, so that I might be delivered with one stroke from such a long run of wretchedness & unbearable exile. Day began to break while I was sunk in these dismal thoughts, & the sailors catching sight of our own ship at anchor half a league away, the captain lent us his boat to take us to her.

There happened to be two English merchants with the captain. When they heard of my plight, they tendered me their good offices, & seeing my clothes all wet from the preceding day, some gave me a suit of clothes, others a shirt, others stockings, & thus dried I was sent to lie on a bed. I was certainly overwhelmed with despair; about two o'clock one of the sailors who had climbed up the fore-mast to set a sail, cried out that he saw a boat adrift upon the sea. The captain came immediately to acquaint me with the news, told me to keep up my courage, & gave orders to bear on it; we overtook it a half hour later, & brought it aboard. The boat was so strong that it had withstood the tempest undamaged, & all my belongings were recovered & not a single thing lost. The sailors had said it was wrecked to have an excuse for not having fastened it securely. This assuredly brought me a great deal of comfort, & led me to wonder at some amazing occurrences in this adventure; first, God had allowed the storm to increase in order to prevent all my belongings from being taken off the boat, because they would have been thrown into the sea when lightening the ship of all the deck load which was next to the prow, & they could not have been placed elsewhere. Second, that He had caused the cable holding the anchor, although thick & strong, to break in order to save us from foundering. Also, that this boat notwithstanding one of the severest storms I have ever encountered, kept eighteen hours afloat without sinking, & finally that of the six ships rounding the Cape together, she drifted towards ours instead of the five others, for if she had been met by one of those vessels we should never have seen her. Therefore I deemed that God wished me to go through all these trials & degrees of misfortune, & so having tested my fortitude through sufferings, sorrows & shipwrecks, he wished me also to experience the direst poverty, to see whether my patience would not fail. But as by His providence He had rescued me from all the others, through the consolations He sent me, in the same way He delivered me from this affliction, the most grievous, especially to a person well-born, who suffers modesty & shame, & would rather die than dare ask for anything, & so He did not permit it to be of more than ten hours' duration.

Nothing of consequence happened during our voyage. We sailed through severe storms but it was March so this was not surprising. We had sailed a hundred & forty leagues without meeting a boat of any sort, when within sixty leagues from the nearest European land we came across two vessels. We raised our flag, they raised theirs, & we recognized them to be French. Our captain being eager to discover whether we were still far from land requested me to tell them that if they would come aboard our ship he would give them tobacco. They readily agreed & even exchanged some of it for wine of Navarre, for they were from Bayonne & were on their way to catch whales in Norway; & this did not come amiss because our cider had been finished four days previously. I was well treated during this voyage; I found the captain as honest a man as I could have wished. Our sleeping quarters were poor, but he could do no more than give up his bed to me. We ate no salted meat. He had four turkeys, a hundred chickens or capons, & twenty-five pigs put on board, so we ate only fresh meat.

The east wind began blowing a gale as soon as the French ship left us, & as it was quite contrary to our course we were three weeks before reaching Dover. As it blew steadily & we were sailing very heavily because the ship was overloaded, I asked to be put ashore. This was on a Friday, & I wished to reach London on Sunday morning or Saturday night, so that I could be there before the predication. While waiting for a fishing-boat to come along so I could go on her & arrive more quickly, I inquired whether there were any Frenchmen thereabouts. A captain who had come two days before was pointed out to me; I went to see him & he recognized me immediately for he had seen me at Marseilles while I was waiting there. I asked for news from France. He told me that the King had appointed commissaries to collect the incomes of the estates of those who had fled & had issued a proclamation to the effect that those who should not have returned on their lands by March next would have them forfeited. I answered that since it was only on condition of recanting I considered it useless, for I could not believe there would be anyone so cowardly as to take such a shameful & criminal course, who, having in the beginning been led

[171]

by the spirit, should at the end listen to the flesh. We were walking along the shore & seeing some fishing-boats going to London, I left him to board one of them &, as I had wished, reached London on Saturday, the seventh of May, 1687. Now as it is likely that my adventures will be over for some months to come, I shall end this little treatise after giving a few reflections upon what I have written.

It is twelve hundred leagues from the last point of land in America to the foremost in England, but I do not emphasize the length of the way as much as the fact that this distance has to be sailed without finding any shelter. Sometimes one can come up to New Found-land [Neuf-Island], an island which is closer to America than to Europe; it is there all the codfish eaten in France & England are caught; but we have always missed it.

Since I found in Virginia advantages which cannot be discovered in the other colonies in the dependence of England, I deem it my duty to state them separately. This I shall do in a few words, for I have already men-tioned them in general. I find there are five reasons for which I prefer Virginia to Carolina, & four for which I prefer it to the other northern colonies. The first is that wheat cannot grow in Carolina because it is too hot. The second, that sheep cannot be raised there for the same reason, & their wool would be more neces-sary than their meat. The third is that they do not grow tobacco, one of the greatest sources of revenue in

Virginia. The fourth, that they carry on no commerce & from all appearances will not for a long time have any produce to freight a ship, whereas Virginia loads regularly a hundred & fifty each year, & through this means can send to & receive news from the whole universe. The fifth is health, for the country is too flat to have good waters. Let no one be surprised that I should speak so positively on this last subject, certainly I would not advise French people to settle in Virginia along the seashore, or in the southern provinces, which are four degrees further away, although there is no want of lands for sale, & as cheap as in the northern provinces, but I feel obliged in conscience to state that the inhabitants I have seen there looked unhealthy & I have met few old people.

As to the northern colonies, the first reason is that they do not grow tobacco; the second is that wine can be made in Virginia in large quantities, & very good, while there the climate is colder than in England, & grapes will not ripen easily. The third is that it is not necessary to spend time gathering fodder during the summer to feed the cattle during the winter or to build stables or hay-lofts. The fourth is that in Virginia slaves & servants can be made to work all through the winter without losing one day & there they have to remain three or four months doing nothing because of the snow & ice.

I also deem it necessary to state the reasons why I prefer the provinces of Rappahannock & Estafort

[Stafford] to the others in the colony. They are three:
pleasantness, health & fertility. For pleasantness, according to my taste, I believe that a country made up
of plains & hills whence spring fountains & streams,
cool in summer, warm in winter, is pleasanter & more
attractive than an entirely flat country, & those very
hills contribute to its healthfulness through good air,
because of their elevation, the good waters they supply,
& the grapevines that can be planted upon their
slopes, for wine is never quite natural on the plains. I
also noticed while travelling about that the inhabitants
are stouter than elsewhere, their complexions clear &
lively, so I wished to know the reason. I was given one
which seemed to me quite plausible; it is, that along
the seashore, & also along the rivers which contain
salt, because of the tide, the inhabitants in these places
are rarely free from fever during the hot weather; they
call this a local sickness; but the salt in the rivers dis-
appears about twenty leagues from the sea, just as one
enters the county of Rappahannock, & those who live
beyond that point do not suffer from it. Monsieur
Wormeley told me also that when he bought Christian
slaves he sent them during the months of July, August
& part of September, to his plantations in the same
county, where they keep well, but if he kept them on
his plantations, although much healthier than Point
Comfort where I spent the winter, they would be sick
during those three months. For fertility I know the soil

to be incomparably better & richer than elsewhere, as I have said before. I could add a fourth reason to the preceding ones, that I know Frenchmen like wine better than either beer or cider, & there are six times more grapevines in these two provinces than elsewhere. These are large counties, the county of Estaford [Stafford] has no limits on the north & west, as I have said before, & that of Rappahannock has none on the West.

As soon as I put my foot on European soil, I found twenty times more French refugees than there had been about thirteen months before, when I left; this brought me great comfort & effaced the horror & shame I felt at the many downfalls I had witnessed while still in France. This is also why I feel bound to give this short account to the public, & it seems to me that if it should contribute to make them settle in the most beautiful & the best country I have ever seen, I would then die happy.

I remained only a fortnight in London & heard that at least two hundred refugees were arriving regularly every day, which led me to believe the same was happening in other places. Therefore I hope God will grant that all those still staying in our kingdom may recognize their fault & that they will also come to make amende honorable in these lands of Reformation, following which they need not be anxious about their establishment, for I maintain that in the country I have just described there are lands not only for those who

[175]

have escaped, but also for all those who are still in France, having been compelled to recant, & all of it is among Christians, for one écu an acre the best & highest priced, & twenty sous an acre along the York river; & should there be too many there & some willing to go further inland, they will be given fifty acres apiece, of very good land.

A sealed & signed copy of the agreement & proposals of the gentlemen who have lands in the county of Estafort [Stafford] has come to my hands, & I deem it appropriate to insert it here. It is absolutely trustworthy, for I know the man who signed it & he is very honest. I do not add those Monsieur Wormeley gave me because they are in English & I could not find anyone able to translate them. I feel a great desire to return to that country & the only thing that might keep me here is that I feel very weak, but let no one be deterred for that reason; I shall give myself the honor of writing to the Governor & the other gentlemen, & shall take the liberty of beseeching the Bishop of London to write also, & if God grants me the grace to recover a little of my strength, I shall go with them. However, I wish to inform them that ships sail usually during the months of August, September & October.

I have just received some news which has brought me great joy; that almost all those of the Religion in my neighborhood, where there were many, left & have arrived in Switzerland; & that at Dye, a town five leagues distant from my home, there are but thirty people left, all the others having fled. For this reason, I will add here, as doubtless there are people of rank among them, that a man of birth arriving in the country I speak of, even if he did not want a grant of land, could easily settle, provided he has thirty or forty pistoles & two servants. The houses cost almost nothing to build, except a few nails; stables are not needed. He can buy on arriving a hundred acres of land, enough for a fine estate, which he will pay for with eight barrels of his tobacco crop; in two years he can easily pay for it with half the tobacco crop, & the other half of the tobacco can be used to buy furniture & whatever else he may need, for this is the money of the country. The money he might bring with him would serve to support him during the few months of the first year, according to the time he arrived, & to buy cattle. The woods are easy to clear, but without taking the trouble to do this, it is enough to buy lands in the territory formerly occupied by the savages; half of it can be ploughed immediately, & they are the best in the country.

As for artisans & peasants, I have no doubt the greatest difficulty will be the lack of funds to pay their passage, for I am sure that once there, they will only have a little difficulty the first year, after which they will live very well, & as I am acquainted with many of the shipmasters, I think I might be able to get them to take off part of the twenty écus a head they have been charging, & perhaps if they were given the largest part of the amount necessary to pay for the food, they could be induced to wait the rest of the year until they could be paid out of the first crop of tobacco.

THE END

Printed, this Seventh of July, 1687.

PROPOSITIONS FOR VIRGINIA[1]

THE proprietors of the land situated near the county of Stafford in Virginia, on the thirty-ninth degree, between the southwest & the northwest dependants of the river called Cittoquan Crecke & the town which is being built named Brenton (to encourage people who propose to move to that country & settle there permanently), make the following proposition: to wit:

To the first who present themselves (to them & to their heirs forever) these gentlemen will sell one hundred acres of land near enough to the said town to build a house, for the price & sum of ten pounds sterling, cash money, & four shillings sterling as a reasonable rent, in consideration of which they will be full owners of the said lands forever.

---

[1]On Nicholas Hayward, see "Eighth Voyage," note 6. The proposition probably deals with the tract bought by him from Lord Culpeper, after forming a company with Richard Foote, Robert Bristow and George Brent, of Woodstock, in Virginia, on January 10, 1686. On the 10th of February of the same year, the King had authorized them to build a town on this location. It was to be called Brent Town or Brentown, and its inhabitants were to be granted "the full exercise of their religion without being prosecuted or molested upon all penal laws or other accounts for the same." This was a clear allusion to the French refugees. The project suffered the same fate as so many others. Brenton remained a name, and is hardly a memory. For a complete account of this episode see *Landmarks of Old Prince William*. Richmond. 1924. 2 Vols.

These persons are assured that the said land is extremely healthful, good & very fertile, producing all kinds of grain, such as wheat, barley, oats & others as in Europe, grapes & all sorts of good fruit, & the waters are excellent.

The privilege of choosing the location for their farms [mesterie] & houses at the above mentioned price will be given only to the first who go to settle there, for the right is claimed to set a different & higher price in the future for the sale of the said lands.

And further to encourage the families who present themselves first, & who do not wish or cannot put up any cash money, but desire to be aided by these gentlemen, they offer to the said persons, to them & their heirs, one hundred acres of land to build a farm & one acre in the said town for a house, & to provide each family with fifteen bushels of Indian corn for their subsistence during the first year, nails & iron-works enough to build the said house which will be 26 to 28 feet long & 14 to 16 feet wide, at the rate of four écus sterling of rent a year for the whole.

And if one hundred acres is too much of a burden, or if it is not sufficient, they will be given whatever they wish, payable in proportion, either in cash, or in rent at the price & conditions set forth above.

London, 30th of May, 1687, on behalf of the owners.

NIC. HAYWARD.

WORKS CITED

ANONYMOUS. *A Frenchman in Virginia. Being the Memoirs of a Huguenot Refugee in 1686.* Privately printed. 1923.

ANONYMOUS. *Landmarks of Old Prince William. A Study in Northern Virginia.* Richmond. Privately printed, 1924. 2 Vols.

ARNAUD, E. *Histoire des Protestants du Dauphiné aux XVI*, *XVII* *et XVIII* *Siècles.* Paris, 1875, 1876. 3 vols.

BAIRD, Charles W. *History of the Huguenot Emigration to America.* New York, 1885. 2 Vols.

——————————— *Histoire des Réfugiés huguenots en Amérique.* French translation by A. E. Meyer and De Richemond. Toulouse, 1886.

BEVERLEY, Robert. *The History and Present State of Virginia.* London, 1705. French translations at Amsterdam and at Paris the same year.

BRUCE, Philip Alexander. *Economic History of Virginia in the Seventeenth Century.* New York, 1896. 2 vols.

——————————— *Social Life in Virginia in the Seventeenth Century.* Richmond. Printed for the author, 1907.

CHINARD, Gilbert. *Les Réfugiés huguenots en Amérique,* Paris, 1925.

HAAG, Eugène and Emile. *La France protestante ou vies des Protestants français qui se sont fait un nom dans l'histoire.* Paris, 1846–59. 10 vols.

HENING, William Walter. *Virginia Statutes at Large.* Richmond, 1812.

[181]

HIRSCH, Arthur H. *The Huguenots of Colonial South Carolina*. Duke University Press, 1928.

JONES, Hugh. *The Present State of Virginia* . . . London, 1724.

O'BRIEN, Louis. *Innocent XI and the Revocation of the Edict of Nantes*. Berkeley, California, 1930.

ROCHEFORT, Henri-Louis d'Aloigni, *Histoire naturelle et morale des Antilles,* Rotterdam, 1658–1681.

SAINT-SIMON, Louis de Rouvroy, Duke de, *Mémoires,* Boislile edition. Paris, 1879.

SMILES, Samuel. *The Huguenots, their Settlements, Churches and Industries, in England and Ireland*. With an appendix relating to the Huguenots in America, by G. P. Disosway. New York, 1868.

STANARD, Mary Newton. *Colonial Virginia, its people and customs*. Philadelphia, 1917. *Virginia Magazine of History and Biography,* 1894 and 1895.

WEISS, Charles. *History of the French Protestant Refugees*. Edinburgh and London, 1854.

WILSTACH, Paul. *Tidewater Virginia*. Indianapolis, 1929.

INDEX

[184]

Durand, René de, 12, 54.
Dutch, 70.

England, Durand in, 18, 20, 23, 58, 69, 77ff, 86; nobles seek
    fortune in America, 110; refugees in, 144, 175.
English lord, 18, 71–72, 77–78, 80.

Fitzhugh, Colonel William, correspondence, 41n; entertains
    Durand, 30, 33, 156ff; befriends Parker, 34; dislikes Durand's
    account, 42–43; Ravensworth project, 40ff, 156–157n.
Foote, Richard, 41, 179n.
France, aid to Canadians, 102; whalers, 170; proclamations, 171–
    172.

Garenne, Marie de la, 35ff, 135, 145.
Gloucester County, 44, 115ff, 128ff, 136.
Goyau, Georges, 37n.
Grapes see Vineyards.
Gravesend, 79, 82, 90.
Green, B. W., 156n.
Grignan, Mme. de, 36.
Guiton, Judith, 98n.

Hall, J. L., 156n.
Hayward, Nicholas, 41, 42–43, 48, 157n, 179–180.
Hayward, Samuel, 41.
Hening, W. W., 40n.
Hirsch, Arthur Henry, 21n, 102n.
Howard of Effingham, Lord, 30, 31, 37, 136–137, 143–144, 147,
    160.
Huguenots, importance of account for study of, 9–11, 18–19,
    persecution, 9, 12ff, 53ff; hope to return to France, 22, 48,
    162n; American propaganda to attract, 21–22, 40–41; aids to,

24, 59, 70, 90; in Carolina, 48, 102; desired in Virginia, 39ff, 143–144, 154–160, 164, 179; Durand on recanters, 58, 62, 64, 175; in England, 143–144, 175.

[187]

OF THIS BOOK five hundred and fifty (550) copies have been printed and numbered for THE PRESS OF THE PIONEERS, Incorporated, New York City. ¶The paper is Glenbourn, ivory wove, and the type is Centaur, 12 point, designed by Bruce Rogers, and *Arrighi Italic*, designed by Frederic Warde. ¶The end-leaf decoration is a reproduction of a map plate by Valk and Schenk, Amsterdam, circa 1700. ¶The designing, printing, and binding were under the personal supervision of Edward L. Stone, at the Press of The Stone Printing and Manufacturing Company, Roanoke, Virginia, U. S. A. Nineteen hundred and thirty-four.

No. 283

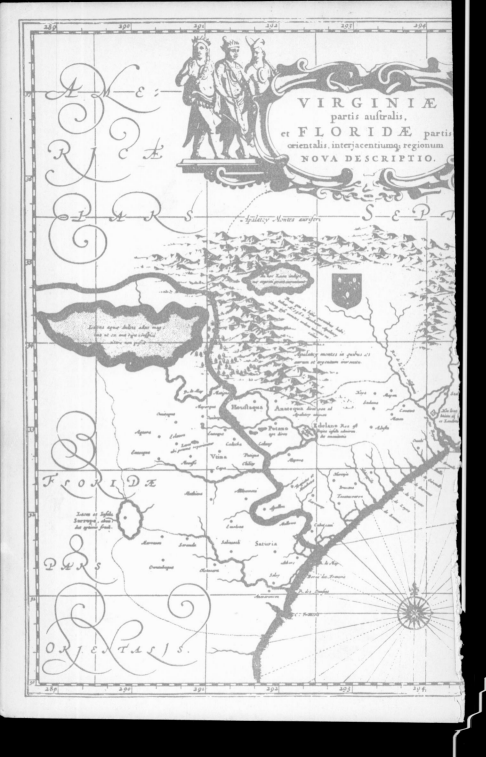

VIRGINIÆ
partis australis,
et FLORIDÆ partis
orientalis, interjacentiumq; regionum
NOVA DESCRIPTIO.